Wretch

Wretch

✦

The Scales Drop

David Cutting

iUniverse, Inc.

New York Lincoln Shanghai

Wretch
The Scales Drop

Copyright © 2007 by David Cutting

iUniverse books may be ordered through booksellers or by contacting:

iUniverse
2021 Pine Lake Road, Suite 100
Lincoln, NE 68512
www.iuniverse.com
1-800-Authors (1-800-288-4677)

Because of the dynamic nature of the Internet, any Web addresses
or links contained in this book may have changed
since publication and may no longer be valid.

The views expressed in this work are solely those of the author and do
not necessarily reflect the views of the publisher, and the publisher
hereby disclaims any responsibility for them.

ISBN: 978-0-595-46018-2 (pbk)
ISBN: 978-0-595-90319-1 (ebk)

Printed in the United States of America

Acknowledgments

First, To The Living God of Israel for His Son, Jesus Christ—nothing without Him.

To close relatives, one who'd encouraged the right answer, to the other that told the truth.

For two people that too much time has passed by, gratitude for their visits is given to God.

Prayers for all in the area who'd helped a slow learner, former co-workers, and for everyone else that had been patient for a former fool to finally see.

Thanks given again to Jesus Christ, for all music made possible—a slow learner was lucky to have had music education.

To two professionals, Dr. S.G., Dr. M.R.

Prologue

Listening had always been a strong point; the head remained bowed while sitting in the pew. The sermon was about watching—something an idiot had not been doing. His Rebukes hurt, the idiot knew it had to happen; the remembrance of loud obnoxious idiot behavior weighed the head down while the village idiot prayed to forbear the hostility of residents in the area.

The four of them walked across the front lawn; sitting on the porch playing his guitar, the smallest of the four stared down in embarrassment. After the other three went home, the runt walked into the kitchen, into the dining room—the guitar had brought comfort from constant chaos. The older man stopped playing.

"Ah have tae ask yew somethin'. Yew tell me th' truth. Wh'n yew'z walwkin' by with yo' friends, dyd yew feel bayd abaut me playin' th' g'i'tar? Anyswer me."

The belligerence in the loud tone combined with hostility on the face—understanding fled, a runt had felt bad only because of playing country music in front of friends.

"I'm sorry, I did."

"Yew list'n tae me ryght now."

He leaned forward, seething anger branded on his face.

"Ah nev'r wawnt ye tae feel bayd abaut me, 'r' abaut yo'self. Ye understaynd what ah'm tellin' ye?"

The runt didn't understand, why someone was behaving as bad as others—the angry stare demanded an answer.

"I understaynd."

He resumed playing, the runt left as Folsom Prison Blues filled the room.

"... while under the car ... He was my hero ..."

"... my grandfather is honest ..."

Very sadly, he may have been honest with others, something important was withheld from his grandson, quote—"yew list'n tae me ryght now." He leaned forward, seething anger branded on his face—"Ah never wawnt ye tae feel bayd abaut me, 'r' abaut yo'self. Ye understaynd what ah'm tellin' ye!?"

Obviously, a scrawny teenager had no clue; what was known at that time; 1. A person behaving like a peckerwood that a teen's mother had stubbornly married was harassing it, 2. A relative had recently died, although not blood, the person who died had been nice to the scrawny bag of bones—"... not Gale ..."—the same pathetic suicidal way his father did, 3. other students, being children who also didn't know, had begun to harass the scrawny runt—the runt at the time didn't know either: truth would be revealed much later.

Foul drama combined with screaming; sparks of anger within a scrawny runt evoked a scream; before the kid gloves could hit the bag, someone had charged downstairs.

"What? You want to hit something? Hit me you little fucking pussy, hit me!"

"... face puffed up like a demented dragon ..."

Seeing the gaze pointed down, "... hate in his eyes ..." ice within cooled the spine, sparks of anger fought against it—something looked familiar in the person's gaze. Knowing the person's profession halted action.

"What's wrong? C'mon pussy, hit me!"

The gaze reminded a runt of old memories.

"That's what I thought."

Escaping upstairs, tires screeched from the driveway as maturity always seemed to be in short supply.

Elastic bands of nerves pulled tighter within the guts, knots of bile threatened to burst within. Punching the heavy bag hadn't made the foolish child grow any taller, just like attempts at hiding behind books didn't stop others from teasing.

"Sisssy!"

"Filthy Faggot!"

Lost blind and in the dark, the foolish child couldn't see why others had picked on him, old memories within the runt's mind began resurfacing during the rite of passage through high school; verbal spitting displaying of affection. Five minutes felt like five years, thirty-five minutes as seconds then back to public displays of affection by other children who didn't know. At the sound of the bell, the runt was already halfway down the hall, at the locker.

A foot raked against the shin.

"What? You have a problem punk?"

After another classmate had strolled over, more public displays of affection, the nerdy runt had to find out a way to stop the spitting displays of affection; notions in the runt's mind had always led it to bad behavior being a temporary fix for a common problem.

"Can I f**k your sister Dave?"

"… judging from your looks, you would need a lot of cosmetic surgery …"

Past tense: when someone is behaving like a peckerwood, the only thing that had mattered was who'd influenced, the individual who'd said this hung out with people that misdirected anger had been channeled toward—some of them behaved like brute beasts; disrespect toward women isn't cool—although some had

the notion, no, I'm sssory sssir, I don't sssleep with men(lisp added).

Present tense; because of a slow learner's bad behavior—sin, sin is deliberate, a mistake is an accident—all of the displaying of spitting affection is forgotten.

Because the wicked want to stir up strife—every opportunity to step on their heels and slap their foul mouths—there's good and bad in all forms of outward appearance, advice—everyone needs to cool it.

Praise Jesus Christ, a slow learner's lawyer—The Name Who Sent Jesus Christ, Respects No one.

Especially not a former brute beast.

Half-slamming the books on the table, it brought someone's attention.

"What's wrong with you!!?"

The temporary fix didn't work for the foolish nerdy runt, it's own snarl escaped.

"Had a lousy day today."

"Join the club."

The snarling made the nerdy runt's teeth begin to grind as knots within the stomach twisted tighter.

Thinking that punching the bag had finally paid off, the tall skinny runt—**"The Hell Marching Man In Black"**—enjoyed seeing some other classmates at eye level. What the foolish blind child didn't see; aggressive belligerent behavior had been adopted, the temporary fix never seemed to work—teeth ground together on a regular basis while sparks of anger seemed to be catching a fire within.

"Just admit it, you have a growing problem."

Actually, not at all—growing in Jesus Christ is a daily, life-long process, Amen.

Opening the door, the grown blind fool stopped.

"What are you doing?"

"He left."

Still not getting it, the stance was the village idiot.

"Who left?"

Although blind and foolish, something seemed to be wrong.

"When did you start smoking?"

No answer was given, the blind foolish child played the new role appointed as village idiot for a few minutes—the answer was caught by the slow learning blind fool. Thinking of all the times being harassed by a peckerwood—c'mon, hit me you little?—the next riddle the village idiot had to figure out, why there was tears instead of laughter and rejoicing; screams from the crib prevented further thoughtful analyzing of this new riddle, the village idiot went upstairs; prevention of teeth grinding meant avoidance of snarls, even a village idiot gets tired of being chewed apart. Seeing the bearded face grinning in a portrait on top of the dresser, old memories combined with public spitting displays of affection by children who didn't know …

… the clock displayed one zero three in red. Leaning in closer, the village idiot watched in disorientation … more confusion at how the clock had disappeared, the heavy bag streaked with blood, knuckles with skin peeled revealed the answer to that … new holes had materialized within the walls, trying to concentrate how to hide them … blood streaked the headboard of the bed, all the registered facts were blending together within the village idiot's mind; the portrait immediately brought the answer as old memories combined with snarling, spitting displays of affection by children who didn't know—a new burning filled the chest and head, sleep fled from the appointed village idiot.

Blind, the burning within did not stop; shifting focus to several girls had embarrassed the idiot on one occasion—the blind idiot couldn't see, teeth gnashed at the burn within the chest and head.

After finishing the day—the idiot escaped by playing idiot video games.

A knock, then the door opened.

"David, get ready. I've made an appointment for you with the doctor, we have to be there within forty-five minutes."

This argument had started since the village idiot's junior year—public displays of affection combined with snarling, harassment from a peckerwood—c'mon, hit me—had made the sparks of anger ignite into the constant burn within the appointed role of village idiot; stubbornly refusing to acknowledge this, the idiot thought someone would leave, he offered an answer typical of an idiot.

"I'm not going."

"David, you had better get off that bed and get ready, your brother …"

The hearing dial automatically switched to a low setting in order to prevent further teeth gnashing, wisely getting ready, no more argument could be made. Children who didn't know seemed to be vindicated in their judgments of psycho, teeth remained clamped all the way to the psychiatrist's office.

"I want you to tell him how you've been feeling for the past year, and all the medicine you used to take when you went to New Haven."

The village idiot offered an answer.

"Don't see the whole point of this, there's nothing wrong with me."

"Don't you worry, I'll tell him."

Teeth ground slowly as the statement rapidly evolved into a snarl, the village idiot wisely kept quiet.

A response.

"How are you doing in school?"

The idiot told the truth, required classes were barely passed.

"Hmm, you think you'll graduate this year?"

The village idiot couldn't help taking the bait and giving back the facetiousness it had learned, mistake.

The relative leaned close, the voice icy, laced with barely contained fury that always served to both humiliate the idiot, and to instruct the idiot to wise up and behave—this was the voice used in public.

The door opened, the voice of wrath evaporated and a smile replaced it, the village idiot shook the doctor's hand rudely then sat—the stare of fury was on the idiot.

The idiot unwilling to co-operate switched the hearing dial on a medium setting while they chatted like best friends.

The doctor addressed the idiot.

"So David. Why don't you tell me a bit about yourself."

The idiot didn't know where to begin: memories from the past began to resurface within the mind causing fuel for the burn within, public displays of affection combined with snarls, harassment from a peckerwood—the cold stare of veiled fury prompted the idiot to answer as best it could.

"When I was growing up and my father had been alive, they'd called him schizophrenic, he'd been hospitalized when we lived in the state of Florida. He was put in the hospital because he shot birds in the back yard, come after us with a revolver, and after we finally got finished moving all over the place, we settled in this area. High school has been good as well, I've gotten punched and teased and I'm kinda pissed about it."

The sarcasm had been added by the idiot in response to the doctor—the notion that he'd understand where this had come from: it flew over the doctor's head, so the idiot just stared at the floor.

Marching through the hallways—**(lisp added) no, I'm sssory, not flamboyant**—the idiot headed to the usual stairwell.

"What's up Dave."

"Same old shit dude."

The village idiot—**Just Two Good ole boys, The Dukes Of Fairfield County would behave like**—did the same thing everyday in high school during it's senior year, at the end of the day, the idiot met his friend—he'd become his friend for covering up the fact of an idiot spraying mace in the stairwells, only displaying affection in return for fellow classmates. They'd BS, doing stupid things, usually an idiot raining abuse on a door that could not walk or talk—town idiot was the right role, most in town knew an idiot when they saw one. A beautiful blonde cheerleader walked by, to the idiot's amazement—she smiled.

"Wow dude! She was hot!"

The idiot grinned.

"She looked at you dude!"

For some reason, the idiot got angry, at the same time, the idiot wanted her to come back—what an idiot.

"No she wasn't dude, she was probably being a jerk like most of them."

The idiot got even more enraged, this was the routine as misdirected rants of anger at classmates, then raining abuse on the doors in the stairwell while the idiot's friend had laughed.

After saying goodbye, the idiot went to work.

Idiot.

Sitting out in the field: the principal called an idiot's name, anger burned within an idiot, the idiot had felt let down by the principal to stop what was just tradition of spitting—waiting while the rest of the names were called, the red and gold caps flew into the air.

The idiot's relatives greeted it.

"F'r a whyle ah thawght ye wa'an't gonna make iyt."

"Yeah, well I did."

A brief flash of anger within the village idiot, then the idiot crossed the field to look for his friend—brief eye contact with a blonde amazed the idiot, his head turned while walking, the idiot also thought about another girl in class he liked—poor dumb blind idiot.

During the summer, the role of village idiot was secured—**although at the time, The Dukes of Fairfield county; present, the Dukes or devils of New Haven county published this chapter with many others**—doing stupid things, the fool should've considered himself lucky, the dumb idiot.

One wise thing the idiot did do, taking advice from a guidance counselor that he didn't like—imaginings of a head exploding was in the nerdy village idiot's mind—the college parking lot, hallway, then auditorium was crossed within minutes, **(lisp added) not flamboyant**—a shift of focus, girls, then burning anger, cold anxiety of what was happening within the idiot's mind: thoughts of children displaying their affection who didn't know fueled the ruminating anger within, focus shifted to a peckerwood(c'mon, hit me) old memories had been uprooted, the focus then shifted to these, adding more fuel to the raw fury within the chest and head, fear at inability to stop this caused the cold anxiety to fight back: most of what the dean of admissions had been saying was lost.

Being a village idiot: communications skills lacked, fear within the idiot due to displays of affection, snarls, a peckerwood had still harassed it when it was angry, which was nearly all the time while a poor poker face that the village idiot could not perceive kept orientation group members away, along with girls—what the idiot's berserk hormones wanted. The shifting of focus combined with raw burning in the head and chest made the village idiot's head hang, the idiot sat in frustration while blue books for math placement exams were passed backward.

Focus still shifted, girls drew the idiot's focus—then anger burned, frustration at why kept the irrational turmoil going within the mind; the first page of the math portion was easy even for an idiot, the second page needed guessing, after that it had looked like Ancient Hebrew to the village idiot.

Passing the blue book forward; the idiot tried talking with a fellow group member, the idiot took the response the wrong way, getting irrationally upset.

The idiot waited while focus shifted to girls, hormones demanded it, but then it got angry, frustration at not knowing why caused the cycle of turmoil within to start—the garbage written in the blue book for writing placement exam had been fueled by the irrational mess within it's mind—the village idiot waited, then one-twoed out of college.

What an idiot.

Walking into the house, the blind idiot didn't realize it's poor poker face, snarls were the response.

"What's wrong!?"

"I'm not going to college."

Response of an idiot.

"What are you going to do?"

"I'm going to work."

Idiot thinking the lecture was over, the hearing dial was automatically adjusting.

"Life is about choices Dave, sometimes we make good …"

The automatic adjustment of the dial was required, the teeth had started to grind.

Retreating upstairs, the idiot felt bad about a relative repairing the holes punched in the walls.

"Ah jus' don't git iyt Dayve, ye git so daymn angry, iyt's lyke ye wanna kill someone."

"Tell me abaut it. I wish I understood it, but ah don't git it either."

The sun beat down on the blacktop like a giant pressing his thumb on an ant; the idiot's mind resembled a fried scrambled egg—a car meant non-hearing of loud belligerence from a peckerwood, no snarls to make the teeth grind. Idiot listening; a strained rev sounded from the engine, being a naïve dumb village idiot as well as lost and blind, the car was pulled half in and out of the exit ramp. Some angry commuters offered the truth.

"Get that piece of shit off the road, idiot!"

Forgetting to put hazards on, more angry drivers honked their horns at the slow learning village idiot. Pulling into a hotel driveway, the idiot asked a receptionist to make a call—poor blind idiot couldn't see that a poor poker face causes beautiful women to turn away. Somehow the idiot managed to make it to work, then called and followed a relative home.

"Pop thayt hood Dayve."

The relative looked under the hood, the idiot waited for the answer.

"Ye hear thayt knockin' from aut'n'under th' hood?"

"What abaut it?"

"Thayt means yo' engine is shot, 'n' thayt real high revvin' means yo' traynsmiss'n'z'awl finish'd'z welw. Mai's welw shut'r awf Dayve. She's awl done."

"We cayn't fix it?"

"A new engine alawng with a traynsmiss'n'z gonna cawst ye abaut toe thausand dollars. Gonna have tae fynd ye a new car."

The idiot went to work: redundant task of burning away unneeded plastic flashing from the finished product—break time, the idiot said little and just listened.

Another co-worker had been talking about Christ—although being an idiot, he'd briefly listened anyway.

"… you don't get ribbons for working for the other side …"

Break time ended as everyone went back to work; cold fear fought against hot anger within, no one seemed to know what was wrong, especially not the idiot going through it.

While driving through a familiar neighborhood, the small stupid Buick the idiot bought with saved money had stalled, smoke hit the idiot's nostrils. Like an idiot, the key—duh—in the ignition switch didn't start the car—the idiot turned his head to the side, someone was running at the car.

"Hey kid! Get outta that car, it's on fire!"

Being an idiot, the person nearly pulling the door off motivated the idiot to get out and see—duh, it's on fire; after running through a familiar park, the idiot stood with a relative, he'd backed away while a relative moved closer. The idiot yelled at the relative to move back, poor dumb blind idiot—the relative did not listen.

Firemen eventually arrived to put out the small stupid Buick from exploding, the idiot just stood there while it's relative argued belligerently with firemen—it didn't matter how it started, it was a ruined mess, the road an idiot's mind was heading toward.

Because the idiot's small stupid car had burned up, the idiot decided to find an extra job—poor dumb blind idiot, following bad advice seemed to harm it while blindness kept frustration along with the cycling mess in it's mind going.

A man wearing a shirt and tie explained the job, the idiot looked around at all the conveyor belts—it's mind was becoming as burnt and ruined as the small stupid Buick was.

Shirt and tie led the village idiot over to purple belt.

"Since this is your first night, just watch these guys and help them out."

The idiot introduced himself—one of the workers looked familiar to the idiot—then the blind idiot climbed onto the chute, struggling, then pulling loose the jam.

"Be careful you don't fall."

The idiot barely made it back to the trailer before parcels tumbled all over the place, a package full of potato chips smashed on the trailer floor.

One of the workers opened a bag and ate.

"You can do that?"

"Want a bag? Have some."

For the rest of the evening, the idiot helped break up jams, and ate chips.

The next night at the shipping company—the idiot walked over to it's newly assigned work area, pink belt.

"This is your supervisor, good luck."

Another shirt and tie demonstrated how to load the trailer, the focus went in every direction—an idiot could still do the job.

The town idiot foolishly tried to keep up with the tumbling packages, the wall looked lousy even to an idiot.

"What is this?"

Shirt and tie had materialized.

"This is wrong?"

Shirt and tie sneered.

"Gee, you think? This wall looks like shit, the packages are going to fall all over the fucking place! Load it like this!"

Because of the role as town idiot; not knowing why such fury built up within, the dumb blind idiot heard something familiar and belligerent in shirt and tie's tone, even though any idiot knew the wall looked bad—so it waited till shirt and tie one-twoed from the trailer before throwing an angry tantrum.

Poor dumb blind idiot.

"Ah jus' cayn't git ov'r yo' car. Dydn't ev'n bye th' daymn thang'n'that sun'v'a'bytch had tae baern up."

The village idiot's focus was drawn onto the car, further making it angry.

"Tell me abaut it. Wish ah never baught that piece'a' garbage."

"Ah knoew what ye mean Dayve."

Thinking that would be it—the village idiot only knew it was lying in a frozen puddle of ice, trying to fix what any fool knew wasn't a good car. Yet the idiot did this because no one else, definitely not a person a stubborn woman had married would help it, the idiot still did appreciate a relative's help. Thinking of the angry person—the cycling mess within began it's involuntary shifting of focus, then chemicals in the brain and body demanded the focus on two girls that had shown nice behavior in high school.

"You think that fyr inspector was right?"

"Haell noe! That 'nspect'r'z'full'a'crayp toe, b'lieve me wh'n ah tell ye thayt Dayve. Thayt fyr dyd not start'n'thayt G** daymn carb'ra't'r, noe question abaut iyt. Whur ah thank iyt start'd from w's thayt G** daymn batt'ry wyr, iyt had a G** daymn short in iyt, 'n'spread ov'r tae thayt G** daymn start'r aut'n'undernaeth. Iyt jus' don't mayke since."

In the idiot's mind—the focus was drawn back to the things that made it angry, back to the snarls, fighting with the person someone had married, stuck back on the displays of affection by other children who the idiot probably wouldn't see again, then ruminating back to someone(c'mon, hit me) brought the idiot response.

"Dyd that faelthy scumbag give ye a hard tyme when ye picked up them parts?"

"Laesn't tae this Dayve. Wh'n we w's aut awn nynty five, G**, daymn'f thayt sun'bytch dydn't crayp aut'n'th' G** daymn layne."

He gave a laugh between the story.

"'Fore ah even picked'iyt up, ah knew thayt aysshole dydn't wawnt anything tae doe with iyt. Ah start'd dryvin' iyt aut awn th' road, 'n' ah said tae myself, G**, daymn, ah bett'r put sum'thayt tin fyfty'n'thayt sun'bytch'n mot'r, caus' ah knew thayt car wa'an't gonna mayke iyt back. We git aut awn th' daymn highway, 'n' thayt sun'bytch starts smokin' lyke haell. Ye shoulda seen hys face m'mayn, he w's starin' daggers at me. Ah look'd at'm ah said hol'dyt. 'N'stead'a'staynd'n thar awl paessed awf, git awn thayt daymn squawk box 'n' cawll a wreck'r. Ah tell ye Dayve, he iys th' most warthless sun'va'bytch ah've ev'r seen. Warks f'r th' G** daymn state p'lyce, 'n' thayt aysshoele cayn't ev'n tell th' diff'rence b'tween hys own ayss'n'a'hoele'n'th' graund, b'lieve me wh'n ah tell ye thayt."

"That daymn job'z warkin' awn me."

"Noe kiddin."

"Hell yeah it's warkin' awn me."

"Noe kiddin."

"Hell yeah it's warkin' awn me. My superviz'r'z'a real prick toe."

"Hay've ye been feelin' laytely?"

Being a blind dumb idiot, the only response was an idiot answer.

"I don't know."

The idiot's relative continued talking, all the way to work. Old memories of a bearded face brought anger within the idiot—the idiot liked that his relative didn't quit.

"Ah w'z lookin' iyn thayt book, 'n'ah thank ah knoew whar we goofed. Don't worry, we'll git yo' car fix'd iyn noe tyme."

"What the fuck is wrong with you? You're loading this trailer like a fucking asshole!"

Standing in the trailer—once shirt and tie vanished, the filthy cursing along with package throwing began.

"What's wrong Dave?"

During the idiot rant, a co-worker had walked into the trailer; the idiot attempted conversation, only filth spewed out. Idiot.

"Don't worry about it, he's in love with himself anyway. You cut your hair. You look much better without that mop in your eyes."

The idiot thanked her—he liked her as well.

"It's almost break time Dave, you'd better hurry to the break room."

Good advice—the buzzer rang—by the time the idiot was finished buying a drink, it's supervisor had told it to go back to work.

Stupid idiot.

"It's cold, isn't it?"

"Daymn'f iyt ain't. Haynd me thayt thaerteen."

Being an idiot with a broken mind, the focus shifted on a neighbor.

"How abaut that dude."

The relative glanced from the corner of his eye: peripheral vision.

"Hah! Ye thank thayt doede'll ev'r git aut'n'und'r'naeth these G** daymn cars? Haell noe!"

Being a lost blind idiot, silent envy was in the heart; a brand new car while an idiot lied underneath a ruined mess.

"Wish ah never baught this damn car."

After Christmas time had passed; audits for employees performance had also passed; a shirt and tie directed the village idiot to a new location, they called it the primary off-load. Although the idiot had been willing to work, filthy rants had spewed out after shirt and tie exited the trailer. The idiot didn't do well enough to load pink belt, the idiot also had a strong dislike for his shirt and tie supervisor. The idiot worked like a maniac, rational hostility from the sorters was the effect.

"Labels UP!!"

Stupid idiot still had a lot to learn.

"Ah jus' cayn't git ov'r iyt. We put …"

While the relative looked under the hood, frustration within the idiot's mind sparked the cycle of madness, repeating thoughts of children displaying affection, old memories, burn against ice cold, the idiot was under constant aggravation without any Truth to support it.

"C'mawn in Dayve, we have tae cawll that guy."

After talking with someone on the phone, a minor adjustment was made, the stupid Buick started up.

"We dyd iyt m'mayn!"

"Noe, ye dyd it. Thank ye f'r doin' that."

"SUPER DAVE!"

The idiot grinned like an unknowing jackass.

Although an idiot, another co-worker had laughed and joked with it, the idiot liked his company and was grateful for his help. True to itself—two co-workers had checked on it to make sure the idiot didn't hurt itself again.

"What's happenin' junior."

"Hi ye doin."

The idiot's co-worker burst into laughter, the idiot kept going like a maniac.

"Slow down junior! Yer bustin' that shyt outta thar like a wild man doped up awn co-cayne! Slow down son!"

The idiot grinned—poor dumb idiot kept going.

"And look at you! You're over there laughing at him! You need to help that boy out!"

The idiot stopped; following his co-worker, the idiot stubbornly listened to him and began to learn.

Dumb idiot.

While the small stupid Buick broke down? times—a younger sibling had a birthday party. What had caused someone and the idiot to scream at each other like true idiots, something just as stupid. Learning by example, the idiot screeched the tires, all manner of filthy rants spewed out, punctuated by punching of the steering wheel—the raw scorch within immediately fueled an idiotic rant at a coward's gravestone—**"ranting in the boneyard"**—he wasn't saying much in return. Then all the red wrath within turned to red branding irons of raw pain within the chest and mind.

The idiot thought about standing in front of the train.

Then it irrationally thought about children who'd displayed affection gaining satisfaction from an idiot's death.

The idiot thought about his younger sibling.

The idiot got back in his stupid junk car and drove back home.

Summer arrived; the idiot didn't resist, the idiot's cold fear also motivated it to take some pills.

The idiot didn't know why.

"… he looked like what my grandfather referred to as a doper …"

At work, heat combined with the process going on within it's mind, the idiot also had joked around with his co-worker concerning a foul mouthed comic—the idiot listened to him, no longer giving place to shirt and ties—provoking their hostility, while sorters laughed and clustered around the trailer where the idiot off-loaded.

A shout went up in the sort aisle—then the village idiot went to off-load metro-lines. The idiot wiped sweat from his eyebrows, with an idiot heavy-metal T-shirt.

Stupid dumb blind lost idiot.

The heat within the building pressed down, the idiot had told his mentor what he would do if shirt and ties kept harassing—a shirt and tie had angered the dumb blind dead idiot to screaming—the entire building had stopped. The idiot's mentor had laughed ever since.

"You ain't gonna quit super Dave!"

"Wawtch."

While working—shirt and tie had barked to the last—the idiot walked to the time clock. The idiot said goodbye to his mentor, who immediately began roaring in laughter. Shirt and tie followed the idiot to the door, snarling at it, the idiot quit anyway.

Idiot.

The idiot saw a doctor.

The same stupid story was spat out.

He increased the medicine.

The idiot walked out.

What an idiot.

"We have to hide …" "I smell something funny …"

Although truth had not been discovered at that time, an idiot had smoked pot in the woods with a former co-worker in order

to speed up the process of 'feeling better'—newly prescribed medicine from a doctor didn't seem to be helping at all. Though the hateful and the wicked would like to use the phrase—"Stared at them under the hat"—to paint a true Caucasian as a vicious hateful swine like them, praise Jesus Christ—bet the wicked thought a slow l-e-a-r-n-e-r wouldn't figure out the stunt they pulled, when publishing chapters of garbage mixed with the truth—praise to Jesus Christ, King of the Jews, Amen.

Well Good Grief, Charlie Brown—a mess when some clowns get a hold of something they shouldn't have, truth of Jesus Christ, Who they do not have.

Nowhere to run, Nowhere to hide.

While working full time at it's job in a plastic factory, the idiot got a notion to move further north-east—the idiot had also heard a singer on the radio, something was in the music the idiot liked, so the idiot would listen to that singer for a very long time. In the northeast, there was a smart relative the idiot had always loved. The idiot thought about moving up there every night while working at the machines. During that month of august, the idiot drooled over a girl with smooth tanned legs, long dark hair on the train ride up—**"Excuse me. Could you watch this?" "For you talking to me, I would jump in the Amazon with lacerated legs filled with pirhanna"**—amazed and glad she'd spoken to it—**"Dave, she's not a scumbag ..."**—poor dumb idiot, a cycle of crazed hormones combined with a mess going on within it's head kept the dumb idiot from approaching and talking to her; the smart caring relative had been good to the idiot—**"... from her model mugging class ..."**—although it's mind was a twisted broken mess—**"... all kinds of sexy in the area ... unlike Stratford girls ..."**—she'd showed it around, and had given the idiot good advice—the relative had also introduced the idiot to one of her beautiful friends from her self-defense class, poor dumb idiot, a mind a mess with hormones crazed.

"… and how did she expect me to have children, by osmosis?"

"… put the condom on my hand to protect it from growing hair on it?"

Past tense—all that stinging sarcasm had been learned from two sources, it wouldn't be revealed till later when the grown up little girls would spread each chapter across the country, in order to humiliate, and destroy a s-l-o-w l-e-a-r-n-I-n-g Caucasian. Because this relative had been smart; present tense a Caucasian has agreement with her, empathy and understanding on why seeing a professional was required—the two sources, praise Jesus Christ, would be revealed, always good to give thanks to God for His Only Begotten Son, not just on Thanksgiving. A slow learning Caucasian apologized, hopefully the relative can forgive a former idiot brute beast.

Praise the Lord, Amen.

While the idiot worked on the night shift—**"… to put her head between the metal pressers …"**—the focus was drawn away from it's job, on the notion of living with the smart caring relative, also on several women in the area, especially her friend—within the mess of it's mind, job performance had lacked. **"… he's behind again!"**

The dumb fool had quit that night.

"I think you're making a mistake kid."

Idiot.

Actually, the only mistake that was made was those people—the ones with the sheets on their heads publishing stolen garbage from a computer. Well good grief Charlie brown,

Praise Jesus Christ—at least we'll know who the garbage and filth belongs to.

Amen.

The idiot rode in the blue van, the loud persistent belligerence in it's ears—"… **remember that bastard that used to live in the green and white house down the road?**"

"**I remember' m…. Ah opened up th' door awn thys van, 'n' looked at that sun'va'bytch ryght 'n' th' eye, 'n' ah said to him, come over here f'r a minute, ah wanna tawlk to yew.**"

"**Ah heard ye been givin' m' grayndson a hard tyme, that trew?**"

"**What d'he say?**"

"**He said, he keeps wakin up m' baby grayndawghter, if he keeps doing that, I'm'onna run'm ov'r … All by myself.**"

"**I believed him …**"

Very sadly, the humiliation would come later, also the knowledge that the body had knew what it wanted all along, the reaction to being pulled by a yoke in an unnatural direction helped cause a lot of hostility, wrath, rage, frustration in a repeating cycle.

Here's a true story—some filthy dukes of New Haven county had watched a town or village idiot for a very long time, how could they not when a relative of his had a loud, thick Virginia/ Texas twang, combined with belligerence, aggression, and stubborn obstinate behavior of his way is best—is it any wonder why no one came close to a suffering idiot, who didn't even know why; all it knew was that foul things had happened to it when it was younger, it got harassed on a regular basis at home and in school, it's mind had been falling apart.

When the peckerwoods of New Haven county realized—Praise Jesus Christ, The King of the Jews, Sent by the

Living God of Israel, Who guided an undeserving fool that sinned, and made bad mistakes, with poor choices of 'friends' away from white trash peckerwoods—they'd published chapters of truth—Praise The Lord, unknown to an idiot's company, He'd Heard a suffering fool under someone's belligerent obstinate yoke—along with garbage in an attempt to destroy, cause chaos, and slander a slow learning caucasian.

At least a Caucasian has a lawyer before the Father, His Son Jesus Christ, Amen.—being dead blind dumb and lost, it laughed not knowing any better—all the way up Northeast. Being a listening gullible idiot—it's mind was filled with blasphemy and filthy lucre.

Dumb dead blind idiot.

The idiot enjoyed the area—the smart caring relative had pleasantly talked with the idiot; irrational clouded thought due to the broken mess of it's mind, what was actually genuine concern for the lost dumb blind fool was twisted and distorted into taking it as an attack. She is a good person to have let a broken dumb blind dead fool idiot live with her.

The idiot started work: the mind's focus had been on how much it liked the area—underneath it was still a ruined mess, many people were friendly to the idiot, —**"... not all New Englanders were rotten ... that vile Fairfield County attitude ..." An idiot would certainly learn—Praise Jesus Christ-just exactly where a grown idiot had learned this vile behavior from**—the idiot also liked the sound in his supervisor's voice.

It reminded the idiot of a close relative—**Praise Jesus Christ, the grandmother had encouraged a lost blind dead fool to attend Christian services, much later—grandmother and grand-**

son Vs … This is the way it is with believers in Christ, and non-believers—the idiot made it through the first day.

Reading through a booklet, the idiot boarded the transit, walked to class.

The idiot was nervous, he told a classmate.

"Theah's nathin ta be neurvous about."

The idiot liked a girl in the class, a sick repeat of crazed hormones combined with a mess in the head started up, causing depressive episodes.

Poor dumb blind dead idiot.

Due to shifting focus, much of important information from the smart caring relative had missed the idiot's ears; pedaling his bike into the city—**"… like an escaped asylum patient banging wildly on a huge pagan gong …" Present tense: although, as some would play a satirical song, 'just too white and nerdy' when an idiot did use music blasting from a junk white Cheverolet as an unorthodox means of communicating to residents—HELP ME!!—several different styles of music had been covered, Reggae, R&B, Soul, Motown, Bluegrass, Heavy Metal; some filthy people who'd gotten a hold of this written garbage, all the misdirected anger at, 1. Fairfield County, 2. Caucasians with sagging jeans; not really caring much about fashion, despite all the times a grown Caucasian nerdy kid has been called faggot, among other names, if you want to wear the jeans sagging down "awf the back'a'yo' tailbone", go for it; a request is made however for all Caucasians, not to be like the filthy peckerwoods that wear the sheets over their heads, blow up buildings, and other foul things they do and love in 'God's Name.'**

Of course, Praise Jesus Christ, King of The Jews—His Presence Guided a poor example—sinner—away from those people;

hence the reason why the truth of Jesus Christ Hearing a broken, yoked Caucasian kid, along with garbage, had been published all over, to destroy—their foul hopes that a caucasian kid would give up like his father and commit suicide—bearded man—thwarted again by the very God those people proclaim to 'love.'

Advice for any and all—Free Will that the God of Israel Gives, listen, live, dress, however you want to, a former brute beast is about the last person to tell any how they should live. What needs to be done, is that those people need to be smacked in their mouths—should they get to a grown nerdy Caucasian, at least the nerd has a lawyer—Jesus Christ—the One who those people claim to 'love'—the idiot had thought of thumping music, the idiot's music taste was still a fool's, narrow minded.

A cop spotted the idiot and called him over.

He looked nervous, "What ah ya looking fawr, Girlfriend? Boyfriend?"

"Girlfriend."

"Thank Gawd."

Again, although just about everyone in America thinks that a nerdy Caucasian is gay—like those people who published someone's messed up life without all the knowledge—chemicals in the brain and body tell a different story that not even an oppressive yoke, combined with foulness early in life could still never change the chemicals and what sex they preferred—this sin—deliberate for reasons still unknown to a nerdy Caucasian—had caused severe symptoms of rapid-cycling mixed bipolar disorder—rare in males.

The wicked—yaaaah!—had known the sources of a Caucasian kid's pain all along—even after everything else had been dealt with first by a professional, then Praise Jesus Christ, Him

Who Can Make those people ashamed of themselves, regardless of what happens to His nerdy Caucasian child.

Amen.

Instead of trying to remember what the smart caring relative had said to the idiot, the fool talked with the cop. After two hours, the dumb idiot pedaled back to the house, ignorantly throwing the bike helmet across the deck.

"The silos opened, the missiles were launched."

How embarrassing that those people, the wicked, had revealed to just about everyone a screaming temper tantrum with a relative—bad idiot behavior: when the same pecker-woods were harassing a caucasian kid just doing his job, praying with some good people—"Keep the faith."—"I keep to myself, brudda."—Jesus Christ's slow learning Caucasian child had seen a printed picture of a mushroom cloud—what was used as a descriptive adjective to convey feelings of rage within a lost, blind, broken, dead, under heavy yoked child—"oh mama mia, let him go" the wicked had arrogantly sung—somehow was attempted to paint a slow learning Christian kid as a hostile, big, bad terrorist.

Whatever happens—a slow learning kid holds fast to the Name of Love—Praise Jesus Christ, Amen.

After the screaming had stopped, and the idiot finished pummel-ing the bag, the smart caring relative talked with the idiot—**"She'd seen what happens when the screaming ...":** All of this rah rah shtuff in the past—screaming like that had reminded a broken blind dead lost fool of the screaming drama that had always been around it—in a few northern states, New Hampshire, Rhode Island, Oswego New York; the wicked obviously enjoy the broken blind lost dead things—they can subvert them to their fool cause—she genuinely cared for the dead fool, she hadn't wanted anything bad to happen to the dead idiot. The mess underneath was now the main focus on the idiot's mind while raw agony increased for the idiot, giving up on living in the northeast. After quitting the job where nice people worked, the idiot left a goodbye note for the smart caring relative.

The idiot was back home again, what an idiot.

The idiot lied on the bed—raw constant agony and pain filled it's mind and chest, paralyzing it. Hours, days, then weeks the dead idiot did not move, brushing its teeth, eating, then lying back down on the bed—staring into space at the ceiling was the routine.

It agreed to go with relatives to a toy store to get the idiot moving.

The idiot wisely agreed to see a psychologist.

In therapy, the idiot knew it was dealing with a competent professional.

Old memories were the focus.

Rain poured down in the humid heat—five minutes later the sun baked down again, making it hotter. The blond runt rode his bike up and down the road everyday before school started.

When school had let out one day, the runt wandered into his father's room. The runt found a shoebox, it had a revolver in it—cold fear made the runt sick in his guts, replacing the lid, he put it back under the bed.

During a short period of time—the runt's father had begun to deteriorate—the runt saw cold cruelty within the bearded man's face. One night, he pulled his son aside—he told his blond headed son vile disgusting things about his mother, about nearly all women, and what he would do.

The runt cried and screamed.

Wanting to find out exactly why the mess was within the head, therapy helped the slow learning idiot understand better what was going on; the idiot decided to go back to college.

It was difficult for the idiot to concentrate in psychology class due to the mess still happening within it's mind; the focus also drew to several girls in the classroom, then on the teacher as the same sick pattern started along with frustration: the dumb idiot didn't know how to talk to women.

What an idiot.

The idiot walked through the hallway with a relative—sitting down, the same boring magazines.

Learning bad behavior, smoking helped take the edge off a grown idiot—the result a new disgusting hawking within the lungs.

"David!"

The psychiatrist opened the door just as a glob of mucus was ignorantly spat into the garbage can.

The idiot shrugged under a hostile stare as everyone sat down.

After giving the doctor what the idiot had learned and knew within it's naïve, ruined mind—the same old story—the diagnosis was manic-depression.

The doctor said it was life-long.

After writing out prescriptions, within fifteen minutes the session was over.

The idiot lit a cigarette outside.

Poor dumb, blind dead idiot.

During school—hormones within the body guiding it, the idiot attempted talking with a blonde. **"... Weston ..."**. Not knowing well enough how to communicate, especially with the opposite sex, what the idiot's hormones wanted—crude manners, or other missed factors must've offended the blonde, she never spoke to it again.

The idiot went home and ranted irrationally, it's mind an angry ruined mess, spewing filthy belligerence it ought not to have.

Dumb dead blind idiot didn't know better.

To the idiot's own surprise, the grades weren't completely as rotten as the idiot had felt. But then being true to it's own learned insanity of self-destructive behavior, the fool began smoking pot along with taking prescription medicine.

Doing this only further wrecked the idiot's mind.

Idiot.

During the remaining month of summer, the idiot quit smoking pot and felt—duh—much better, yet the fool also stopped taking medicine.

"Hangin' With The Homeboys"—"Just make sure you use protection when you take her back into your room."

Since those people; peckerwoods with an attitude who think sheets are a fashion statement, hooo, yaaaaah! Aaaaaah, pinky extended—made a former brute beasts' personal life public—Truth mixed with garbage, the garbage a result being without full knowledge for all to see: Being the white boy in the suite—because the majority of black kids in high school hadn't spat on a grown up minnow; with the exception of a few peckerwoods, 'can I fuck your sister Dave?'; like good people, peckerwoods are varied as well—the white boy, broken and fouled up, lost, blind, pissed off and not knowing just exactly who he was really pissed at yet: what experiences were known at that time: 1. Several Caucasians, male and female, boys and girls, children who didn't know, just like a white boy in college were treating the white boy foully, 2. This had happened since middle school, 3. At home, foul moods were manufactured by someone a stubborn woman had married, who just happened to be a cop,

harassment from the loud stubborn woman in the form of a cold, sharp, samurai sword edge of snarling aggressive belligerence, the person she'd married—again, had also given his best—C'mon, hit me—4. The redundant, unpleasant past; at the time of hangin' with the homeboys, the foulness in New Hampshire due to a loud stubborn woman's—sin, for reasons still unknown at the very present—neglect had not been brought to the surface of the ruined psychotic mess that was a grown infant's mind, neither was the yoke from someone else discovered yet either, so one can imagine the kind of lunacy of a head completely wrecked with a body that's chemically going crazy for the opposite sex addled with marijuana and malt—kissing beautiful young women isn't supposed to make someone full of rage, then 'onions in the eyes', especially not when it's body wants to chemically continue—someone made an error—sin: all hostile words were written, directed at Caucasians in the area, due to lack of truth, Jesus Christ The Jew, King of Kings—so all that rah rah shtuff, written and directed at people in the area was displayed by sheet wearing, white trash peckerwood wearing, pinky extended, yaaaah, aaaaah—people.

Rah rah garbage written in the form of a conscious stream; a misdirected angry rant typed on a computer: first, present tense, no excuse for bad behavior, a slow learning, nerdy Caucasian kid will answer to his Lawyer, Jesus Christ: despite all the garbage written, fuel for the peckerwoods who let the plogs out, who published all these chapters—oh, dear—they knew exactly who'd been paining the Caucasian, who it was really angry at, they'd thought for sure to manipulate, direct the foulness at their intended target—anyone other than someone who won't put a sheet on their head and be like them.

"I think we need to 'mother him'...."

After settling into the dorm room: other incoming freshman introduced themselves.

"What up dog."

Curious, the idiot walked into the next room.

They introduced themselves.

They rolled blunts.

The idiot smoked with them—more suitemates walked in, they also had blunts, the idiot smoked with them as well.

They put on music, the idiot was burnt—the music stopped.

The idiot got to know them, he began to like them.

Then the idiot went back to his room.

The next day the idiot went into the city.

On the way back, the idiot missed the shuttle.

Lost—two hours it took the idiot to walk back to campus.

A suitemate offered to smoke, but the idiot was too tired.

Later the idiot woke up and talked with his new suitemates.

He was starting to like them even more.

The idiot put on a tape he'd heard about, his friend from high school had played—the Gravediggaz.

Another suitemate walked in, he looked at the Caucasian idiot strangely, then smiled.

Unsure of how it happened, the idiot had drawn female attention.

The idiot went with the girl to her room.

He nervously kissed her—the same sick pattern, the idiot's hormones wanted to continue.

Rage, then the idiot was in raw pain and didn't know why.

Stupid blind idiot—the root of sickness hadn't been found out.

The idiot being fouled up, the idiot's wrecked head thought about all the girls—**"… would've given more than an education …"**—the body wanted and could've had—something was wrong within the idiot's mind.

The idiot hung around his suitemates, he enjoyed their company—like an idiot, he smoked pot with them at their pace—autistic mind traveling through outta space was the result.

Stupid dead blind idiot was destroying it's ruined cycling mind further—the idiot still liked his suitemates.

In a smoke filled haze; the stupid idiot sat in an empty room, the semester had passed by.

Pain that couldn't be measured crushed the idiot's mind, it ripped a void within the idiot.

He sat alone.

He missed his suitemates.

Lying down on the bed, the gaze was at nothing—which was exactly the sum left of the idiot's mind and within it's chest, except pain exacting it's fury due to pot smoking like a professional.

The idiot walked to a nearby house after rising with effort.

Sitting on the couch, a relative flicked through the channels.

In an ignorant, misguided attempt to make a lost broken blind dead gullible idiot feel better—some ramblings went on about something that happened long before an idiot was even thought of.

"Ye know, we would'a won thayt war, m'mayn."

"No kiddin."

"Yeah…. them southerners could handle them rifles, don't think they couldn't …"

Wait a minute, hold it. If someone that; 1. Worked for thirty six, or thirty seven?—years for the federal government, why the???? would this same man, teach about something that hap-

pened, long before an idiot that actually listened—although at that time in all honesty, not to the right person; an idiot has a lawyer in the present, Jesus Christ The Jew—to loud persistent, stubborn belligerence, 2. "I'm not impressed sir, that you worked for the federal government", "Well, ye oughta be!"

At that time, a blind dead jackass snickered—present, a former brute beast wishes he could find the black woman that a belligerent person had aggravated at the DMV and apologize to her; present, a grown up kid in the prime bridles the tongue—so much damage, ramifications of foul belligerent behavior for so many years by a relative, then a kid had previously behaved like a brute beast, most likely compounding all snickering town gossip that, oh dear—that fool is just like that belligerent?

At least the present slow learning kid has Him for a lawyer; those people, the dukes of New Haven county who published chapters—?

God respects no one—especially not a former brute beast.

Concerning any who want to label a broken, slow learning kid, that has nerdy characteristics, Pinocchio—at least the slow learner has a lawyer, Jesus Christ—Someone Who most seem to be turning away from.

Was it circumstances—a father, s.g.w. in a West Palm Beach motel, someone else with pride and arrogance—"Yew List'n tae me ryght now"—that made a former child with blond hair that could easily occupy his own time, on his own—into the monster that the wicked first tried to recruit, then attempted to scapegoat against the very body—federal government—that someone had arrogantly, loudly proclaimed he worked for? Since most seem to want to put their own label on a kid who had sinned, made mistakes of his own—wasn't a mistake that chapters were published all over, the Ku Klux Klan, Aryan nation sissies who are going to be slapped across their mouths—better to Fear The Holy Awesome Mighty Powerful Terrible Feared Name—Who both kinds of those people will know—He Is Their Judge, The Living God of Israel—He Loves Judgment, only He Lives Forever, He Is Invincible—not the Aryan nation.

Now was it a mistake that a kid—Praise Jesus Christ, The Name Made Flesh, Amen, The Son of God Will Be Glorified, no matter how much those wicked and hateful people—KKK, Aryan Nation resist, Without Christ, The Name's Terrible Face Will Be Against them, Nowhere to run, Nowhere to Hide: was it a mistake on a kid's behalf that, no—despite filthy teaching by a stubborn belligerent relative, and brute beast behavior; present tense, if any should get distorted thinking, believing that a kid did not get disciplined by God, restructure your thoughts, His Discipline hurts, yet required for helpful, positive loving behavior, unlike those people, KKK, Aryan Nation, preaching hate, violence;—a kid wouldn't put a sheet over the head?

Say anything you want—praise Jesus Christ, His Lawyer.

In too much pain to care—the discussion brought an argument, then an accurate response.

"They were fighting for slavery!"

"L'I'll be G** damned'f'that's what iyt was! The G** daymn North attacked us first!"

"But we still won!"

Although it's mind was a scrambled mess from effects of pot smoking and raw pain, the idiot smiled.

"Ye cayn't tell'r'nothin m'mayn."

The focus drawn onto the empty void within caused pain to rip fresh through the idiot's mind, the idiot got up and trudged back over to it's own house, lying on the bed.

The idiot stared into nothing.

The idiot shut his eyes.

Present tense: although several foul things had happened in a slow learner's life, Praise Jesus Christ—forgiveness, and forgetting is important. If a grown up nerdy Caucasian kid can get over; violent disgusting assault—not sex like many in ignorant pop culture would believe—think New Hampshire "Remember me?", two suicides, several years of peckerwoods of all kinds harassing it, a person who'd helped an idiot in a kitchen getting murdered—you might not like this, Caucasians need to get over the civil war, Africans have to cool it with the slavery—if this isn't humiliating enough, a kid had been a slave for many years—think "his will not let him go" a crappy song if asked for a personal opinion—the very reason why a nerdy Caucasian, praise Jesus Christ, has to slap some kluck kluck klanners and Aryan bambina satanic women.

Just advice—knowing Jesus Christ is important—again, free will.

Knowing, a kid isn't the best example either, however it's good to be generous with anything learned for the benefit of others. Or any, regardless of outward appearance—can communicate—'rap' some brand new forms of filth at a former brute beast. A sheet has been made; a nerdy Caucasian that loves to read, loves vocabulary is always interested in hearing new labels of filth, and marking down points for names, labels, or judgments by others. This is exercising of free will, praise the Lord, and freedom of speech, God bless America, not Amerikkka.

Guess a slow learner was also the last to know that being Caucasian in America means the requirement is to put a sheet over the head—should a former brute beast be punished anymore because of a loud mouth? Mr. Big Stuff, yaaaaah! Who did those people think they were? Watching over the years, the wicked couldn't believe that a Caucasian wouldn't side with them.

At least a slow learner has a lawyer, Praise Jesus Christ, Amen.

Lying down on the bed, dead, lost, broken and blind, in constant pain from it's own stupid pot smoking, someone—hit me you little?—had kept up the routine of aggravation and harassment, snarls with a sharp edge had fueled this, because it had been amusing to stir up drama; the same old song, only with a different peckerwood. Instead of trying to help the dead thing lying on the bed for fourteen plus hours daily, bad behavior only continued; someone had a bad day, a dead thing had the only choice of lying on the bed—church would've been the best answer.

What's worse: hateful and self-absorbed, or dumb and broken.

They're both dead.

Just when the pathetic dead thing had returned from the northeast, twice; the routine of brushing teeth, eating, occasionally showering started up again while the mind was still a mess. The dead thing, when not lying on the bed, had to avoid snarls that served to aggravate—hours of sleeping, staring into space, writing filthy twisted foolish garbage on a computer helped the dead thing gain some relief—sometimes it had played music, some of the heavy metal, some that reminded the idiot of his former roommates; hours turned to days, to weeks, to months—it had repeated it's self destructive cycle. After getting help within an out-patient program, it fell back into pot smoking like an idiot; a psychiatrist was found in the city for the idiot.

In therapy with medicine, without pot smoking and drinking—the dumb pathetic idiot felt better, at least for a little while.

Ready to work after a long sleep of death in depression, an old friend had helped the idiot find a job at a restaurant.

A woman with curly brown hair smiled at the idiot, leading the idiot back into the kitchen.

It's brain had been seared with pain, isolation in the death sleep of depression, it was afraid to talk to anyone.

Someone gave the dead idiot a job of cutting bread.

A blonde haired woman smiled and said hello.

The dumb idiot barely said a word.

She smiled again then walked away, the idiot liked her.

Being an idiot thinking it could keep up with the dishes, it stubbornly worked without pause all through the first night.

The idiot went home, then fell asleep.

A few days later, the idiot worked by itself in an irrational panic, the co-worker who trained it was gone.

Someone had approached it and talked to it.

Then he'd helped the idiot clean up the kitchen at the end of the night.

"Yuh have to tek de linen out."

The idiot liked him, only he'd helped the idiot at the end of the night, so the idiot talked with him. While wheeling garbage barrels out, he stopped.

"Yuh have a southern accent mon. Where yuh from?"

Obviously, some peckerwoods had hoped to use 'irrational distorted thought' of an idiot "… defending himself …" writing when they published each chapter to stir up hatred and trouble between Caucasians and Africans—especially trying to cause trouble for a nerdy Caucasian that refused to put a sheet over the head, praise Jesus Christ.

Irrational thinking went through the idiot's head, then the idiot answered truthfully.

"I live in Stratford."

"Yuh sound like yuh from Texas."

The idiot didn't know any better.

That's what the wicked love—idiots that are lost and blind, who don't know any better, again, to subvert them to their cause. Should a nerdy Caucasian kid have the opportunity to separate a kid from a peckerwood bully hanging all over it—Praise Jesus Christ, it has to be done, sowing the good seed, at least the truth that there are good and bad in all types of people—all that other ignorant garbage needs to be buried. Advice for kids—don't listen to that propaganda garbage that 'friends' can sometimes put in your ears, also watch for orange flame tattoos and a shaved bald head, the hostile belligerence just oozes from the unnatural bambina woman's eyes as 'he' looks for his next target to pick a fight with. Here's your daily bread Mr. Big Stuff—a live dog is better than a dead lion—yaaaaah!!

Praise Jesus Christ, King of Kings, King of The Jews.

"Ah guess I've been hanging around my grandfather too long."

"There it is again mon. Too 'lawng'."

The blind idiot followed Raymond out to the dumpster.

"Watch de sticks."

Being an idiot, the reason to watch the sticks would eventually be found out.

Up in an idiot puff of ganga smoke, summer passed by.

Like an idiot—pain seared into the brain again, the mess within the mind started back up.

The blonde woman sat with the dumb idiot, talking to it.

The idiot felt better, he liked her even more.

Pain was in the idiot's mind; he couldn't tell the difference between joking and serious.

What an idiot.

Toward the end of September, the idiot had wrenched his wrist carrying out trash. During this time, the idiot knew everyone in the restaurant, he'd also picked up some Spanish from other workers as the idiot still liked to listen—most if not all like the idiot, repeated relapses to pot smoking seared the idiot's mind combined with the mess of manic-depression symptoms had clouded what little rational thought remained.

The teasing began.

"How did you do that Dave?"

"Use the left hand, it feels like someone else is doing it."

The idiot turned red, then walked over to the dishwasher.

After smoking—the difference between joking and teasing vs. serious was still lost on a lost blind idiot.

A waitress walked in, the teasing continued.

The idiot grinned and turned red, then went back to work.

Idiot.

"… he seemed to know when to stop teasing …"

Raymond had gotten tired of teasing, however, some did not—an idiot had helped another co-worker out—being a blind lost dumb dead idiot, an easy target for a tail to be pinned on a donkey.

Wintertime had arrived while sixteen hour days worked on an idiot.

Once again, pain branded itself across it's depressed mind, it put on music to make itself feel better.

Raymond turned up the volume, the kitchen had filled with Buju Banton's voice.

The idiot talked with Raymond; stubbornly following, he'd stopped teasing about the 'injured' wrist.

From all the double shifts, severe symptoms of manic-depression—the idiot decided again that his cowardly father was right, the idiot did want to die. **"Crash and Burn".**

Instead, he voluntarily checked himself into a hospital.

After waiting hours for medicine, the idiot took some—he'd talked with a black woman and enjoyed the nurse's company.

Then the idiot got tired and fell asleep.

After spending three and a half days in one hospital, the idiot was transferred to another.

The idiot went to group therapy.

They allowed smoke breaks.

A nurse had aggravated the town idiot, behavior reminded an idiot of someone else, but didn't know who.

"Don't let that get to you D. One day at a time."

The idiot had liked Gordon, he'd praised the Lord, he seemed to be about getting better and back out again.

Soon enough the idiot was released—without any 'injury'.

The idiot was looking for Someone.

"... celebrities ... movie stars ..." Since hormones, again—(lisp added) no, I'm sssorry sssir, I'm not chemically attracted to men! I don't point, I don't ssstand with my hand on my hip—pato. Comprende?

Also, a grown kid doesn't put a sheet over the head—again, just advice to other ethnic groups—Don't behave igno-rant—those people that put the sheets on their heads, who also smeared all these chapters across the country, to blame a nerdy book smart, but not people smart Caucasian. Because those people—sheet wearing, pato, sissies are ignorant—brute beasts.

The Living God, Respects no one.

The idiot went back to work glad to see everyone, especially the waitresses.

A grin greeted the idiot.

"Hello smokey Joe."

"Hello Raymond."
"I saw Buju Banton at Toad's place."
"Good show?"
"He did all his songs."
The idiot grinned.
"Lot of smoke?"
"Lotta Hate!"
"Smoke and dreadlocks everywhere mon!"
"That's cool."
The idiot talked a bit longer, then went back to work.

The idiot sat in front of a meat-grinder computer—it still had to find a way to vent the rage burning within—what an idiot, it still hadn't figured it out yet.
The phone rang.
The idiot picked up and listened.
The idiot sat on the bed in shock.

Sick twisted nerves stirred up in the guts, it reminded the idiot of another wake just before high school.
His relatives were there.
Raymond was gone.

Stopping at a relative's house—a greeting of affection made the idiot feel sickened.
The idiot drove across town, punching the steering wheel, clawing at the back of his neck in disgust.
The idiot kneeled before the TV—after punching the headboard—the idiot kneeled there.
Then the idiot just closed his eyes and wept.

The idiot went to a professional.

The old memories were made present.

The young couple had lived in different places. They had one blond boy. Snow had piled high over the windows, where they lived was cold during the winter months. Being an infant, it still had some aware-ness—looking at the bearded man's face, he stayed away, when the screaming began, the runt hid himself upstairs.

The wintertime had passed—for reasons unknown, the boy had stayed over at different houses in the neighborhood: during the summer-time, a girl in the neighborhood had come over to watch the boy.

Her brother hung around the boy too much.

"… laundry detergent …"

He led the runt under the porch where no one could see.

The runt's face was mashed into the gravel under the porch—ready to scream, a hand covered his mouth.

"Dana."

The idiot sat in the office.

It seemed life wasn't challenging enough for an idiot, its mind was a mess—this resurfaced right after his friend had died.

Once the idiot had finished speaking, it did something right—listening to clear rational advice.

He grinned giving instructions: "Okay Dave, here's your next challenge …"

Although while working, others were calling the dumb fool with the accent still present in it's voice, faggot, sissy—remind-ing it of high school, the fool had worked calmly and coolly as best it could—some girls had stopped into the shop. The idiot had of course liked them, there just seemed to be something still stopping the fool from relieving its body.

He stood in front of the idiot, arms folded.

"I can give you anything you want …"

Although he seemed to know what the idiot wanted—The Light Within an undeserving idiot Stirred—the idiot smiled nervously and went back to work.

Someone had mentioned to a former brute beast about 'helping' an idiot publishing his book—too bad the idiot wouldn't find out what the hateful already knew—"Oh mama mia, his will not let him go …"—although, praise and thanks given to God The Father, although His Name Is Terrible Very Strong Powerful and Fierce, His Son Jesus Christ Is His Love—something the darkness comprehend(ed) not.

The dumb idiot wouldn't realize what the wicked had done until thanksgiving—then the fool would finally find out, just who exactly had been paining it for several years, to quote a big and fat white rat—"I think we need to 'mother' him …"

Being an idiot, it sat on a barstool by itself, a piece of the puzzle that made up the mess within the idiot's mind fell into place.

The idiot drank; stupid irrational behavior, the very opposite of what the professional had commanded it not to do.

Once again amazed—a tall beautiful blonde approached the idiot.

"Hi. I'm Janine."

"David, nice to meet you."

Listening while she talked—still amazed she would speak to an idiot, any attempts not to look failed.

Poor dumb idiot—timing was off, too broken and smashed to pursue.

What an idiot.

The summertime arrived, more cruel timing, the idiot was still a mess—a cheerful brunette had been friendly to an idiot, it smiled stupidly at her, it's body liked her while negative, self defeating thoughts immediately ruminated around in it's fouled up head. Walking through the parking lot, the garbage barrel immediately stopped, spilling contents all over the place.

"Watch de sticks mon."

The idiot still didn't see.

"Just like I'd been angry for being a virgin, he was angry because he was gay."

Sadly, the anger had been mis-directed, someone—sin, deliberate pride and arrogance of attempting to shape someone into their 'graven' image—put a yoke on an idiot. All things in the past, combined with bad behavior, assortments of peckerwoods harassing it, the lunatic 'thinking' or ruminating of thoughts by children mistreating it in high school—lunacy, but the anger was craftily misdirected. Someone else's whip tongue—samurai sword of cold edge—had dumped toxic waste, "… her bad day becoming mine …" It seemed that bitterness against a grown idiot's bearded father for committing suicide over twenty years ago, was being dumped on an idiot. Jesus Christ is Forgiveness, it is only that the truth needs to be told for the benefit of many others. Too bad a kid suffering couldn't see at the time who was kicking it, at that time, the grill-man a kid had worked with had reminded him of children's mistreatment. Obviously, the rational shred of sanity prevailed while working in the restaurant—it had been shocking that someone "… grillman …" a co-worker wasn't behaving like others had in a grown idiot's life—Tunde, Frank, Raymond, Gordon; sadly, some hateful peckerwoods used this misdirected garbage thinking written down on a computer—"… staring down at the sink …" to try to fuel their filthy cause, 'smiling face', "I can give you anything you want …" "Anything you write is genius."

Present tense—God forgave a grown kid, so all that garbage, misdirected anger is cooled. Thankfully, a kid in the present has

a lawyer, Jesus Christ; gossiping is hateful on any scale, small or great. When the wicked are praising something a grown kid has done, it is time for careful self-examination, quiet, meekness, being watchful—letting Jesus Christ bring about revival within. The continuing struggle, denying the wicked their reaction desired, impossible without Jesus Christ—the wicked had revealed about an idiot, who misdirected anger was at—which is why revival had to happen.

There are Caucasians, then there are those people; although they'd humiliated a grown kid on many levels, attempted capture and planned to murder—"No one would ever believe it." Smiling face replied—this was the trial, making up for a brute beast drawing filthy symbols that the wicked, dukes of New Haven county love, offending nice people in a local diner: dealing with stereotypes concerning Caucasians, this one acknowledges first to his lawyer, Jesus Christ of sins; stupid, yet the trial with the hateful makes up for it: speaking the truth, Jesus Christ can save your soul. A Caucasian keeps quiet after everything that had happened, neutral is about the best a slow learner can give for now. It's better to be quiet and pray. Maybe not all Caucasians are full of baloney, just 'fake friends', 'smiling faces' who knew all about a brute beasts' book being published chapter by chapter. Parasites disguised as roommates had latched on to take a bite, a slow l-e-a-r-n-I-n-g Caucasian had to move out of a nearby city, after finally, a relative told the idiot the truth about someone—"Yew tell me th' truth ... 'r' abaut yo'self ..."

The chemicals in the body still know what they want, natural women,(lisp added) nnot men! Someone's—sin—loud belligerent aggression, with intimidation, caused a lot of people 'full of baloney' to latch onto an aggravatingly slow learner.

Praise the Lord, He made an help meet for Adam.

Amen.

Not long after, the idiot switched jobs again, something still seemed to be in the way of the idiot: the clinging symptoms of manic-depression ripped apart the mind, tearing further the empty void within the chest. Taking focus off of inner pain was cigarettes mashed into arms—while working at a temp job where some had aggravated it, the idiot began slicing arms using a butcher knife due to wrath. The idiot found a job at a bookstore; it kept in quiet pain to itself—because of some hostile heavy-metal it sometimes listened to, along with fury that a poor poker face didn't always hide—the idiot was put back in the stockroom away from the small percentage of pompous arrogant customers. An idiot easily provoked to anger wasn't a good choice for customer service, so it worked in the stock-room.

It had been amazed, yet fouled up twice with two girls it had worked with; it had asked another woman out—politely refused. The idiot had felt mildly better about itself for asking—it was still a fouled up mess.

Poor blind, dumb idiot.

A year and a half later, the dumb fool started somewhere else. With encouragement from a close relative—the idiot was encouraged to attend Christian services.

Poor lost blind dumb dead idiot—it was suffering in raw agony and wrath from being kicked, so it couldn't see **"We do church differently!"** that a poor poker face drove good people far away.

That summer of the new millennium, the idiot worked at a book warehouse. During the first five months it worked there, it's crude learned manners had kept people away from it, it had a void from agony caused by loneliness ripping through it for years, the medicine temporarily helped an idiot while loneliness kept the pain right on it—it did it's job, but kept to itself.

The mess of clinging ruminating symptoms of manic-depression, pain, wrath, frustration and isolation that it couldn't seem to get itself out of, affected it's job performance. It complained and ranted, poor dumb blind idiot.

Still blind and dead, and in pain.

During the month of February, someone had been assigned to work with the idiot in red aisle. The idiot not trusting anyone, had asked the co-worker if he was using the schematic.

"No."

The idiot went back to work with a grunt.

Unsure of how it happened, the gullible lost blind idiot had become friends with his new co-worker, because someone had been friendly to it, the idiot followed.

"… he didn't seem like natural enemies, white wanna-be gangters …"

Concerning that: several people have incorrectly called a Caucasian, black—since this filthy disgusting corrupt world only looks at outward appearance, obviously Caucasian—just one that still won't put a sheet over the head. Concerning the 'white wanna-be gangsters', you can wear your clothes, put on all the ghetto accents, listen to all the Jay-Z, hip-hop you want to, just don't behave like a peckerwood. Since this world is nothing but filth and corruption anyway, not sure if any advice will be heeded by any. A slow learning kid can't wait till Jesus Christ Stands upon it, till then, the tongue is bridled shut.

Some people, those people: KKK, Aryan satanic women—decided to draw the entire country's focus on an idiot.

That's fine, Praise the Lord Jesus Christ, a Caucasian's law-yer.

At it's apartment, the blind idiot lost dumb dead thing wrote more filthy vile disgusting things, chapter by chapter—it did this because it's other alternative was slashing it's flesh with a paring knife, pressing cigarettes into it's own skin, raw agony and pain battled constantly within it's own ruminating mind while loneliness tore the void wider within.

Poor dumb blind lost dead idiot.

After work the idiot went home, hearing the phone ringing. During that time, its former supervisor at a shipping company had lived below the idiot—this made the idiot furious, the idiot wanted to carve initials within the fool's face.

Picking up the phone; an idiot heard loud belligerent bambina woman complaining; loneliness was ripping the void further within the wrath filled idiot—the crafty bambina woman had promised the idiot to meet with one of the girls she worked with.

Instead, the bambina woman aggravated the idiot to wrath, slamming the receiver down.

"... seems women only love scumbags, wanna-be gangsters ..."

"I'll give you her number ..." "... but she only dates black guys ..."

What had followed: think cabinet scraping—was brutal slashing of the flesh; the icing on the cake was a former supervisor, your attention please: conveyor belts, 'super Dave!'—only a shred of rational thinking remained in the provocation to homicidal wrath with a knife; hearing loud angry belligerence combined with a slamming receiver: what was known at that time—1. a twisted broken thing had been lonely, 2. it had learned to fill the empty void within with belligerence and aggression, 3. Its body knew what it wanted, but a mess going on in the head, 4. The twisted angry enraged thing was tired of phone calls after work—someone got the notion to dump toxic waste on the angry thing, intentionally provoking it to wrath and extremely unhealthy levels of homicidal fury. The thing remembered foul treatment, by several self-righteous Caucasian kids, white wanna be gangsters in the thing's broken ruined mind—, like the twisted dead thing carving it's arms from factors such as raw pain from years of suffering, loneliness, hormones out of control combined with the ruminating cycling mess going on within it's head—they didn't know.

Sadly, much later, after some peckerwoods pilfered chapters of truth mixed with garbage, in an attempt to capture a sinner against the Living God of Israel, attempting to destroy already a bad example of a Christian, slander with every filthy line—those people, "White trash peckerwoods Will"—had arrogantly known just exactly who had pained a grown up kid.

There's a difference between Caucasians, and white trash peckerwoods.

Twisted with fury from being constantly kicked, lost, broken, blind, dead, and in the darkness—the knife—"**... thought of all the people who'd hurt it ...**"—gouged violently across the shoulder; old memories of all the people who'd hurt it motivated the sharp blade to part the flesh, blood gushed from the deep wound, the idiot paced and ranted full of all manner of vile filthy speech out on it's balcony where it lived, cigarettes mashed brutally into the skin weren't felt, the lost blind idiot was gnashing it's teeth in the outer darkness of hell, infernal fires burned within the suffering dead thing.

Eventually, the idiot realized that it was really fouled up, after the insanity of self inflicted laceration ended—the wound sprayed blood all over the bathroom. A relative was called: in the car on the way to the emergency room, a fable about cabinet scraping was made up—stupid, the dumb thing probably needed to be hospitalized again.

"… it was hard for my grandfather to come up with a lie … an honest person …" Honest just like the very people that published someone's book, a former brute beast—a 'smiling face' that wants to be friends. The words of a pastor in church—"Satan's not gonna come at ye roarin and terrifying, he's gonna come at you as your friend."

After the entire country humiliating a slow learning kid—the best people are going to get is neutral, present tense.

The only friend desired is a Christian woman, girl, female.

Oh, that's right, the world is telling a slow learner what his own body wants. Not to rap, but in the words of a late rapper, "… F@#K the world …"

Smile—Jesus Christ died for all, even a slow learning Caucasian.

The idiot sat in the waiting room with a relative, a blonde nurse walking by caught his eye—duh, too bad it was a fouled up mess.

The idiot watched the doctor, with the exception of a few idiots, most doctors are smart, that one was no exception.

"Did you do these?"

Learning by example, a fable was made up about them.

The doctor administered anesthesia—pinch, burn—then sewed the dumb dead idiot up.

The idiot stayed home from work the next day.

At work: the stupid blind idiot hung around his co-worker, play pin the tail on the jackass—kick the braying idiot till it behaves the way you want it to. More of the filth just kept braying out from the brute beast jackass—poor dead dumb idiot.

A result of this—"**… hate cloud …**" "**Vin and Dave vs. the three …**"—the supervisors, who before did not have a problem with the dead broken idiot—now they did.

What an idiot.

Summertime had passed: peckerwoods with an attitude full of disgusting hatred decided to crash jets into the World Trade Center, murdering thousands of people.

The idiot went home, if it had known how to pray, it would have.

"**… pray to Allah …**"

Obviously, past tense an idiot in the dark—present, praise Jesus Christ—Free will, if any doesn't want to hear the gospel of Jesus Christ—how bout the weather? Not crashing a jet into a building, putting a sock over the head—or a sheet for that matter either.

When angry 'female dogs' decide to cause trouble for a former foolish donkey brute beast—they need to be slapped like 'female dogs' that they are.

Dumb dead blind idiot.

One month later: the idiot screwed up again, cracking, the dumb fool loaded the cases wrong.

The supervisor had rightfully demanded why the cases were loaded improperly, the fool couldn't help snarling. After a talk in the office, out the door again.

What an idiot.

Out of work, months had passed. Instead of trying harder, it's idiot focus had been on the vacuum within it, and the blasted mess that was left of it's mind, the idiot could not get itself out of the outer darkness full of teeth gnashing it was stuck in.

It hung out with its co-worker.

"Hey slut, you still writing that book?"

The idiot replied stupidly: somehow the conversation turned to God.

The idiot listened: within the idiot's mind, he'd thought maybe Jesus Christ could help.

The idiot kneeled down along side his co-worker.

"Heavenly Father,"

"Heavenly Father,"

"I have sinned against you."

"I have sinned against you."

From the depths of hell—The God of Abraham, Isaac, Israel, and David Heard an idiot's cry.

Despite being a poor example, kneeling before Hosanna, a Caucasian will stand before men—Praise Jesus Christ, not ashamed.

A week later—the co-worker had introduced the idiot to another Christian.

The idiot was nervous—the people in the church welcomed the new Christian.

"You'll like the pastor Dave."

A taller man with glasses introduced himself.

"Hey Dayvid. Nyce to meet yew buddy."

The idiot grinned, it couldn't help it, that sound had been in it's ears nearly all it's life.

"… grandfather's slow and heavy, his brother's sharper and faster …"

With the pastor, Praise Jesus Christ—an actual accent without all the filthy lucre, blasphemy—things being taught that shouldn't be taught—ironic since someone worked for the federal government? years.

During service, the idiot was slowly beginning to feel much better—His Presence Stirred within the idiot.

The idiot liked hearing the sound without blasphemy and filthy lucre combined with aggressive belligerence.

The idiot knew he had to keep going back.

The idiot hung around his new friend, they played video games: the idiot still had a long way to go, it still hadn't gained sight—filth spewed from its mouth at losing.

The idiot talked with his friend, he was giving good advice, concerning children in high school—their judgments of psycho vindicated, the misdirected anger was still ruminating in the idiot's mind.

"You have to let that anger and hate go, when you hate someone, you're a slave to that person."

The idiot was trying—the idiot knew he had to go back to church.

"… a good ole boy wasn't ever going to be a slave …"

Just to make sure: some peckerwoods, 'good ole boys', dukes of New Haven county—hate should stay, and die with them.

A Caucasian leaves all the Judgment to the God of Israel—He Loves Judgment.

Praise Jesus Christ, Amen, a wretched slow learner's lawyer.

Two nights later, a guest pastor was in the church, they were having a revival.

The idiot's friend had been drawing on a piece of paper: the idiot was listening, hearing about Love, Everlasting Life, Humility, Meekness, Kindness, Charity: the guest pastor suddenly began to shout—the sermon had been about people following a sports figure's behavior, his reasons to the public.

"… Don't look at me! I'm not your role model! AND HE'S RIGHT!!!"

The pastor's voice filled the entire church—the idiot had the classic look of surprise—then the idiot bit his tongue and began to elbow his friend, he was starting to laugh.

The idiot liked to hear about Jesus Christ—one day the idiot hoped he'd be able to tell the Good News.

But the idiot still had a long way to go—couldn't see the whole picture yet.

Idiot.

Although Christ Who Died and Rose Again Heard an idiot's cry: a blindfold seemed to be deliberately kept over the idiot's eyes—the dumb donkey wasn't watching the sticks; at home it still heard loud womanly complaining—stumbling blocks the idiot tripped over many times, pulled in another direction than of Christ's—Love.

"Flesh Vs. Spirit" "… going into places, shouldn't have gone in …" "… Good Grief, Charlie Brown …"

Due to hormones that didn't slow down: 1. The only knowledge concerning physical relations was gained only in theory from books—nerds love to read; considering that a grown up nerdy kid had foolishly asked his 'best friend' with the 'smiling face' about that kind of, most likely, baloney—a kid didn't have any opportunity to find out—someone put a yoke, choke chain on it, the head fouled up, the body knew what it wanted: however, surrounded by angry, loud, belligerent women—two to be exact, 2. No excuse for sin, friendly advice to any—He'll punish and discipline, it doesn't pay, 3. The favorite kind of eroctic videos a lousy, undeserving idiot used to watch—Good Grief—Straight: unlike what every gossiping little female dog in the is country now thinks, so get smacked and slapped like one, Bi-racial of all kinds, been called pervert in addition to all other

kinds of filthy communication produced in homes and school systems: no excuse for sin—the former foolish brute beast certainly got disciplined—when God does it, it hurts, yet it's required to correct. Again, although a fool example, most bigots full of hate that wear sheets usually don't watch bi-racial eroctic videos: dividing truth from fictional garbage is awesome.

Not to entertain pop culture, just an important lesson in stereotypes, unless, like a former fool, someone is glued to watching eroctic videos—that certain myth about cousins—"Duhh uh huh huh, the ***insert filthy racial slur*** walk like that because they got huge ..." was started by white trash peckerwoods: upon talking with someone—the angry belligerent loud bambina woman who mentioned a girl she'd worked with quoted, "They're just like everyone else, some have it, some don't"—this had been the girl the loud angry belligerent woman had wanted a lonely broken fool to meet: only the loud woman's stubborn prejudices got in the way of a kid having at the very least, someone to talk to and maybe starting to like—instead it was more provocation of an idiot to anger, that led to seven stitches in the upper left shoulder due to toxic waste dumping filled with belligerence: seeing the scars and burn marks, the hateful, white trash peckerwoods who no one likes, not even a Caucasian nerd—fell all over themselves to try and separate a fool from his Master, Jesus Christ. Bribery with their daughters for a lonely fool was the evil ulterior motive, their personal gain, a trained, devil indoctrinated foot soldier to carry out their filthy plans—an idiot brute beast had been trying to rid himself of all the foul ideas it had picked up, toxic waste that had been dumped on it.

Praise Jesus Christ, although the loneliness has in the past fed into depression, He Makes it tolerable in the present: sadly for a former fool, he couldn't see the company he'd been in,

"Hooo, Yaaaah!"—the dizzy duo was thankfully stopped. For the peckerwoods—no, I'm sssorry (lisp added) a grown slow l-e-a-r-n-I-n-g nerdy Caucasian kid has no desire to see and prove that myth that you peckerwoods started—maybe if you peckerwoods misbehave, you can go to prison—"Ryker's Island"—to actually see for yourselves, yaaaaah, aaaaaaah!

Praise the Lord Jesus Christ, it is much better to be alone praying to Him, than to have what the body wanted all along, daughters offered as bribes to side with evil, regardless of how many gossipy little ***ches say—"... like those vile soap operas my grandmother watched ..." "He's gotta be gay"; it isn't any-one's business in the first place, but some filthy white trash peckerwoods published some garbage along with truth—Jesus Christ Is Lord—in hopes to turn what's become, really always has been a nation of gossipy little ***ches against a Caucasian, not a white trash sheet wearing peckerwood—before a slow learning Caucasian could defend.

Not that a Caucasian—Praise Jesus Christ—has to be a pleaser of this world, filthy, evil, and corrupt: the Author of the sixty-six books of the bible says so, Praise The Living God of Israel.

Let a Caucasian answer to Hosanna, Jesus Christ, The King of The Jews, for his own sins. Unbeknownst to the company a former fool kept, the Master Had Heard—it was a personal choice a suffering thing had made up it's mind to do, one similarity to a stubborn aggressive relative; words of a pastor come to mind with a loud roaring style from the church pulpit concerning all of a former fool's behavior—eroctic videos—"Don't look at me, I'm not your role model!" A caucasian has been wrong many times, done wrong—concerning the words of that pastor, Praise Jesus Christ—when a slow learning Caucasian shares that advice for any and all, 100 percent correct—more advice, follow Jesus Christ, open up a bible—that's the free will a slow learner is trying to exercise.

In the present—due to spending several years in blind dead hell—a slow learning Caucasian is neutral, trying not to say much, all that former rah rah rah loud behavior is shaming enough 'Rapping'.

Not the greatest example, like someone had said to the former dead thing lying in hell, "One day at a time D."

And like the words of someone else who'd most likely been a fool,

"I know that my Redeemer Liveth, In the latter day, He Will Stand on this world."

Praise Jesus Christ.

So you know, not a lowly wretched slow learning nerdy Caucasian, The Lord Jesus Christ, The Name Made Flesh, Praise The Lord.

The idiot worked at a gas station, playing some of it's former music, only much less being that the dumb brute beast donkey had to interact with customers. The idiot heard in a sermon—how do you react; hearing and not seeing, the idiot tried to react good for evil; but there was and always will be peckerwoods of every outward appearance and kind. Snarls from the undeserving idiot had escaped; not watching the stumbling blocks—the idiot had aggravated a cop. Still not seeing the company who it hung around, combined with hearing of loud belligerence, pulled into two directions at once.

The idiot's mind was still slowly recovering—Jesus Christ Want(s)ed His idiot child to Witness His Work.

What an idiot—very undeserving.

"Sweet Southern Roots by the grace of God."

Sin is deliberate, a former idiot brute beast will answer to Hosanna, Jesus Christ for sins. A former fool tripping over a stumbling block, stick—garbage had poured out—the lovers of this garbage had cleverly and craftily pilfered chapters from a computer—sin—let a former fool answer to his lawyer, Jesus Christ. The garbage belongs not to Caucasians, but white trash peckerwoods with an attitude, yaaaaah!

Just advice—free will is a gift from God, it's what separates man from brute beast, Praise Jesus Christ: truth can be painful, especially for a former fool—due to many errors, foul events, long term suffering without Jesus Christ—yokes had turned what had been a kid, into something ugly, creepy, and non-pleasant.

To any, regardless of your free will to choose Jesus Christ or not—don't behave ugly, creepy and non-pleasant: those people, white trash peckerwoods behave like those characteristics, yaaaaah!

Not telling any how to live; a slow learning Christian in the present, taking it one day at a time D; Just advice—don't behave the way a former brute beast did either, sin, bad mistakes, errors of the kind of people it chose as 'friends'.

Actually being a former brute beast, the reason for 'someone's' shocked disbelief, when the Light—Jesus Christ, King of The Jews Who Died For All—Guided a former brute beast away from the wicked—darkness, which comprehend not the Light. Revival in Jesus Christ; it starts within, showing a former brute beast the folly of blind hatred.

There are good Caucasians, then the white trash pecker-woods—good and bad is in all forms of outward appearance, it's just that lovers of garbage who 'let the plogs out', pilfered garbage, chapter by chapter—dukes of New Haven county who think they've found a slow learning Christian kid guilty.

Praise to the lawyer Jesus Christ, Amen.

Although Christ Heard and slowly changed His idiot child, the idiot still took his pills—they seemed to be good for helping an idiot sleep, something that had always fled due to people harassing it from when it was little.

Being used to waking at four thirty in the morning, the peckerwoods had still aggravated it—because of stumbling blocks, as well as hearing filthy lucre and complaining, along with some of its own garbage within its mind—the same stupid repeating idiot cycle motivated it to find employment elsewhere.

Undeserving idiot—it still couldn't see the sources that had caused the cycling mess within it's mind—the undeserving fool couldn't see the stumbling blocks.

What was more pathetic, the game of pin the tail on the donkey then kick it, or the dumb donkey that still couldn't see who was kicking it, taking pills that probably were never needed in the first place.

Idiot.

"Wake up slut! All you do is sleep when you come over!"

Tired from waking up at four-thirty, sometimes taking pills—the donkey stopped over his 'friend's' house with his girl-friend, Sara …

Although a forty-five minute drive, the hills looked nice in the fall.

The undeserving blind idiot had never been in that part of the state it lived in—it still liked how the land looked.

The idiot applied for a job.

Then it started working, a dangerous job loading and unloading plate glass onto trucks—dropping a sheet could mean amputation of arm, hand, tank your pick.

The still blind idiot drove and worked. Although not very big, the idiot got used to lifting glass—public displays of affection that can be frequent in retail motivated the idiot to lift.

Other workers had begun to like it, they joked with it and teased it.

"You're a powerful little motherfucker."

This had made the idiot feel better.

Although the drive was long and the pay not worth it—it did not want to hear peckerwoods complaining like bambina women because: the coffee tastes like dirt—Dunkin Donuts or Starbucks; an idiot has to card because if it does not, the store gets a fine—if you want to smoke cigarettes like an idiot, the carding has to be done.

Yet because the game of pin the tail on the donkey continued, sometimes it did behave badly like a bambina woman with the braying complaining.

"Hmm mmm, mmm mmm mmm, I hate this bar."

"It was time to bring loyalty back to Christ ..."

Repeat of the pastor—"Don't look at me, I'm not your role model!" Let a Caucasian answer to Hosanna, Jesus Christ for his own sins—sins are deliberate, mistakes are accidents—drinking in a house of mirth, bar, wasn't a mistake, it had been deliberate and foolish.

What many didn't realize; country music played in a car, Johnny Cash sung in a bar, due to a job behind a cash register; 1. an idiot that cried out to the Master—the God of Israel is the Master, His Mercy is Jesus Christ, someone that peckerwoods with an attitude don't want to know—Praise the Lord for Free Will, 2. An idiot had still needed to grow in patience for all the job requirements of retail being spat on—complaining about the coffee. Although an idiot shouldn't have even joked about it, the 'big D special', rat poison and ground glass in coffee

would've never have happened, best to put the peckerwoods being slapped across their mouths in prison, Ryker's Island is the recommendation; if you need smokes, gird thy loins as a man, or else a kid needs to see ID—(lisp added) no, I'm sssorry sssir, unlike what everyone else alssso now thinkssss, a kid doessn't sssleep with men—there's Free Will, good positive communication in Christ, or filthy ignorance because a grown up little white girl spews because an undeserving Caucasian is doing his job by asking ID before vending cigarettes: due to everything that had happened to a former blond headed runt, the undeserving fool really had been trying to let go of who he'd perceived to be angry at—caucasians in the area, all the negativity had stuck in the mind in rumination—Praise Jesus Christ, God's Forgiveness. At that time, an undeserving Caucasian fool had seen a reaction of dislike upon another caucasian's face when playing country music; someone had also obstinately, arrogantly insisted that plenty of people in the area listen to country music; being slow learning, drunk and foolish singing Johnny Cash or Lyrnrd Skynrd at a bar, full of drunk people, not "bar trash", Free Will, you want to drink, go for it—the filthy communication shouldn't have been a shocker. That's why drunkenness isn't good in a Christian's life; the slow learning fool had found that out.

Being shamed, so a former idiot had written—"It was time to bring loyalty back to Christ"

Poor fool—still couldn't see the stumbling blocks, the sticks were tripping the natural man, full of garbage and sin, from moving forward in the right direction, growing in Jesus Christ, Amen—fool had forgotten someone's advice—"watch de sticks mon."

When a Christian stumbles over a block or a stick, shame at all the garbage pouring out is revealed.

Although a slow learner, Praise to his Lawyer, Jesus Christ, Hosanna in the Highest.

Sin is deliberate, let a slow learner answer for his—the source of the sticks would be revealed, hooo, yaaaah!

A co-worker had quit, shortly after, someone got the notion to switch hours to third shift—the grown idiot kid lasted another month, then the idiot quit, other wise it would have not lived much longer, take your pick, arm, leg, hand.

"Parallels in his life and mine ..."

"... picking on my grandmother ..."

Those parallels are: a woman who dumps toxic waste on her children when behaving foully, the swine, dukes of New Haven county knew this: they'd watched carefully a grown kid, when trying to separate a kid from his Master, Jesus Christ, the King of the Jews. What was said,

"I think we need to mother him ..."

Just like when it was realized first by the wicked, then by a fellow condo resident—'oh dear' he's not putting a sheet on his head.

"I think Dave needs some recognition."

Frustration: to see a younger sibling ever side with swine—those people—is anguish. He doesn't have to be Christian, just don't side with peckerwoods, those people. Again, no one really likes them—not even a nerdy Caucasian—a former brute beast.

Praise Jesus Christ, Amen.

"Parallels ..."

The angry woman got the notion to date someone that remarkably resembled a?—that's why it was later said to the younger sibling—God loves you, His Son Jesus Christ is proof: all that loud, angry, belligerent—sin—infantilizing—bad mistake that is being repeated—behavior—that isn't loving behavior, that's something else, even a s-l-o-w learner can see.

Past tense: when sitting at the dinner table in a room full of strangers—it's upsetting to a brute beast that people who care or know nothing about a kid, especially when picking on a relative that had given the right answer among many wrong answers and choices, the right answer of attending Christian services: presently, the wicked sheet wearers also have to be countered concerning that typed angry rant in that chapter.

"More like the Long's, than the Cutting's."

Present tense, the only one who is important is Jesus Christ, a slow learning Caucasian kid, that likes to read, the bible is the first pick, just trying to live on day at a time, despite being a poor example, i.e. poor attendance at church. Neutral toward others is about the best that can be done for now.

Identity in Christ—it really isn't anyone's business—this world can't have a kid's soul, it belongs to Jesus Christ.

You err, you get slapped—poor example—just like those people are being slapped in the mouth for their sin.

Unable, and not wanting to control the behavior of others—a slow learning nerdy Caucasian does the best to behave. That's why the nose is in the bible.

The idiot found another job much closer to home, the area it grew up in despite a coward that had moved it all over.

Although the Master—Jesus Christ Was(Is) with it—it was still blind, pulled in the opposite direction the donkey needed to go.

During work, bad behavior, sin started: being gullible along with being cleverly manipulated and led—bullied—still no excuse for the bad behavior and filthy lucre's sake in the car, 'dizzy duo'—yet it happened.

Eventually the idiot went on vacation all the way down to the Blue Ridge Mountains—the blind dumb undeserving donkey couldn't figure out why no one liked it, so it went on vacation.

It's body had really liked some girls down there, it got the notion in it's mind that it was in the right direction, along with hearing the pastor's voice teaching the Gospel of Jesus Christ, Love, Charity, obedience, Revival within—a similar sound with far different content had always pummeled the donkey's floppy ears non-stop for a long time: so the sound that didn't belong in the dumb donkey's voice picked up steam.

What the dumb donkey didn't understand while on vacation—'ye need tae be reprograymmed, Dayvid'—was the nervousness of a relative, especially when the idiot liked a girl behind the counter, the relative had grinned.

Getting those old feelings back again, the anger seemed to be allowed to be misdirected away from the source—now the accent was with it, back in the area it grew up in.

Still no excuse for bad behavior—sin—the donkey knew it's own braying mouth kept good people of all kinds away—angering good people and neighbors it had grown up with, before a coward decided to quit, only after terrorizing his blond headed child.

This is why even a dumb braying donkey would not quit and give up—Jesus Christ commands to fight the good fight—it was also beginning to see who was kicking it. Being a dog drawn to it's own vomit along with being pulled in an opposite direction of Christ and Love, it wrote stupid filthy chapters, misplaced anger—chapter full of garbage, ranting with unnatural bambina woman complaining.

The donkey did not figure that out yet—it put it on a computer.

"Way down in the Blue Ridge Mountains", "... He looked nervous, his brother grinned knowingly ...", "Voice sounded

like cotton candy ..." "... red flags ... looked at someone else passing ..."

What was known at that time: 1. Tired of being spat on, something was still wrong, 2. Not paying attention—let a former brute beast fool answer for sin against the Living God of Israel, Praise Jesus Christ—strivings about the law were viewed, most likely the reason some peckerwoods latched themselves onto a former brute beast, stupid, foolish, 3. At that time, in one of life's ironies, it hadn't been the old traditional norm—due to perceived opponents who a former brute beast believed were kicking it: that had been where the former brute beast had got the notion to 'rock the boat', 4. Seeing that—duh, people in the area don't like country, tired of the same old song, perusal of music brought back good memories. Stevie Wonder had reminded a brute beast of when it had blond hair, his late father's friends, Tunde and Denise had come to visit in some of the states the blond headed boy's father—bearded man—had moved him to—Rochester, New Hampshire, Wakefield, Rhode Island, Oswego New York: Port St. Lucie Florida might have been too far, but Tunde and Denise had always visited when up north. The reason at that time, why sometimes twangy blue-grass, other times, Stevie Wonder, Reggae blasting from the car in complete idiot, loud, lunatic rah rah behavior—yokes other than Jesus Christ were still attached to the brute beast—poor dumb jackass still couldn't see. His body had liked the girl; the rage at coming back—sin was allowed to continue.

One of the dumb donkey's favorite things: heading to the music store. Walking through the aisles, due to someone "knowing best", it had heard just about every country song you can imagine—tired of hearing the same old song, the dumb donkey saw the grin. A grin of it's own formed on his face: it wasn't always bad.

The blond headed runt stood on a rock, he began to aggravate the elderly in a convalescent home—still a child, it learned aggravating behavior from his bearded father, when he wasn't being aggravated and terrorized himself. Tiring from doing this, he remembered his father's friends, they were stopping by to visit—they lived near a great lake.

Picking out a record … the grown idiot grinned as Stevie Wonder belted out Sir Duke … *he couldn't wait to see them, screaming and shouting had always seemed to chase him.*

The boy grinned when he saw them.

"Hello Tunde!"

"Hello David!"

He grinned at seeing them both—Denise had skin light as the boy's, Tunde was dark. He wanted to leave … the grown idiot didn't want onions in the eyes—there was already too much bambina women behavior going on around it to last ten lifetimes.

"Go fuck yourself motherfucker!"

Various garbage about comparisons of southern and northern women, angry misdirected garbage; rants typed about a bad date, fool writings about an actual church girl who did like the dumb brute beast—obviously, a woman and a dumb brute beast isn't a good match, only in the present, a slow learning Caucasian is tired out, if God provides, Amen, if not, Praise His Son Jesus Christ anyway—still not a good example, if any don't like this, awww, boo hoo. Obviously, a failed date—if only the Caucasian could've rewound time with knowledge in the present, boo hoo.

The former idiot had typed about telling a former friend about Jesus Christ, he wouldn't listen—duh, with years of learned garbage still spewing, no wonder. Present—neutral, silently praying, keeps the mouth shut in public as much as possible.

Although lovers of filthy garbage, dukes of New Haven county with the stunt they pulled, "I think Dave needs some recognition."—publishing garbage for all to see, since God forgave a slow learning kid, no more rah rah loud behavior: despite all the gossipy rumors that some dukes had orchestrated, inexperience—"What do you know" a Caucasian snarls somewhere in a bar: you're right female dog, nothing, so follow an example and keep your mouth shut before you get categorized with those people and get your mouth slapped like them as well, punk—bad example, at least a kid is honest about it—not learning how to communicate, being; not African, Caucasian—nerdy, shy, thoughts of a northern girl with long dark hair and blue eyes makes a slow learner think without 'injury'.

A slow learner had hung the head in hope the girl knew Jesus Christ, let a former idiot answer for his own sins: the Author of the Bible commands against sexual sin, fornication with a non-Christian woman. Sin is deliberate—a former fool already has enough sins to answer for.

Concerning a church girl, a former fool had listened to idiot gossip about a Christian woman—presently why a former loud mouthed brute beast keeps his own mouth shut.

A shame most others don't do the same—yet taking the positive out of the negative, it's good that most in this world hate and revile a grown Caucasian—Praise Jesus Christ, a kid can't be friends with this vile, corrupt wicked world.

At least He'll Stand on it.

All that gibberish concerning the color of a former fool brute beasts neck—Praise Jesus Christ, fool brute beasts die.

The idiot was—big surprise—unemployed again; going to a temp service, the idiot was found a job.

Never expecting it, the idiot had come to like nearly all the people he worked with, one exception, the donkey brute beast avoided.

Eventually, the donkey hung around two of its co-workers.

Driving through town, the idiot had noticed that some were just as mixed up as the donkey was, confederate license plates were on some of the cars. The idiot put on Stevie Wonder, his supervisor reminded him of someone, the idiot was also glad to have a girl sitting next to it, most looked through it, or shouted filth at it.

"What? White people don't listen to Stevie Wonder!"

The undeserving Caucasian donkey didn't care, it brought back good memories that kept it from getting aggravated.

The idiot's passengers had been nice to the idiot, other co-workers had tried to help the idiot get relief, but it was too scared, someone had drilled something into it's head that was against what it's own body wanted.

He liked other women there as well, what an idiot.

Then, like an idiot, job switch.

After another job switch, looking through the paper, the idiot found another shipping job.

The donkey idiot: blind and asleep, it had still complained at times like a bambina woman, behavior it had learned. The idiot didn't have a problem with any there, some it did avoid, others it learned from: the idiot was asked to pick it up, there could be no mistakes for the job—duh, soon enough the idiot quit.

What an idiot: there was actually several bambina women there that it liked.

Idiot.

Walking into the temp agency, the recruiter found the idiot another job; back up north where it had loaded glass.

The idiot went for an interview and it was hired: stupid dumb donkey brute beast fool had no idea.

It needed to drop the accent like a virus.

"But what we don't need is power abusing peckerwood punks hiding behind a badge, they're no better than the thugs they're putting away …"

"… send them to Ryker's Island with diamond hard thugs and criminals for five minutes and see who's nervous."

The need for obvious northern, close to NYC style of cold directness is the choice: those people, white trash peckerwoods with an attitude, swine, dukes of New Haven county that published stolen garbage, in hopes of painting a s-l-o-w-learning kid as a fellow neo-????? lover—making their phone calls with smiling faces: somehow, cops had pulled over a kid doing his job—just like the cops—the smiling face had hoped to make the kid angry, swaying him to leave blue for red, ultra extremist red: where they got the notion, must've been hacked from a computer: concerning who gets sent to Ryker's Island, how bout the right people, those people—who stole garbage from a brute beasts computer.

Present tense; although tired and broken—no matter what happens to a former brute beast idiot, praise the Lord Jesus Christ, a kid's lawyer. Hearing every kind of filthy communication, this had also served as a lesson to a former brute beast: he'd offended two nice people at a diner, the medicine was a fiery trial by the hateful and wicked—the same who published garbage, the same who'd also tried to find a way to threaten, terrorize, and kill a grown-up kid that had behaved ugly, creepy and unpleasant, like a brute beast.

Any can spew more filthy communication—Jesus Christ is the lawyer. The loud mouth is stopped—neutral.

One day at a time.

For the first three and a half months, everyone seemed to be watching it—stupid dumb idiot undeserving donkey—it had learned loud belligerent behavior. A smiling face was pulling the string, absorbing personal information without giving back, the stupid southern accent it had picked up on it's vacation still sounded.

There were good people there, the undeserving donkey had prayed with them; at the same time, the braying mouth seemed to be landing it in water filled with bloodthirsty sharks—smiling faces.

Jesus Christ Was(is) with His grown idiot donkey child, because of loud braying behavior it learned, the Light Guided the idiot away from them—sharks wanted the idiot's blood.

Stupid dumb jackass idiot.

"... Ignorance is taught, by uncles, older brothers ..."

Present tense—no matter what is said, a nerdy slow learning kid would have to defend for the rest of life—confession and acknowledgment of a former brute beasts foul behavior to God, He Sent His Son Jesus Christ, for all—even a brute beast gnashing his teeth in hell; 1. Sin doesn't pay—the result of loud stubborn rants of filth in the past—makes it triple times harder to convince a younger sibling of revival in Christ, that God is real, Who Made all things, His Mercy Is Christ. A former brute beast, donkey fool has that guilt, hence the expression, sin doesn't pay, aware that yeah, a s-l-o-w learner is a sinner, 2. Every eye shall see, every knee shall bow, every tongue confess, that Jesus Christ is the Lord, 3. Frustration at taking it one day at a time with knowledge of flaws, imperfection as well as acknowledgement of former foul behavior, not being an articulate speaker the truth that it's important for any and all to acknowledge God's Son while the body is alive, 4. Although a younger sibling has said to a relative—"He's not the same per-

son"—it is still a hope that a younger sibling will listen—a former fool paid dearly.

Praise Jesus Christ, a grown slow learner is glad of God's mercy.

His peace is the dew on the grass, His anger is the roaring of a lion. Praise Jesus Christ—His anger is but for a moment.

Unfortunately, foul teaching, this because the company a former fool idiot donkey, gullible brute beast hadn't realized—God Had Heard, praise Jesus Christ—a dead gentile, God breathed Life into a suffering dead thing. Along with hearing the right way in church, some 'smiling face' was teaching foul things: good grief Charlie Brown, trusting someone holding the football; hooo yaaaaah!

Praise Jesus Christ—only after being buffeted, humiliated, seeing spray-paint on signs in town, where someone got that notion: the dizzy duo was stopped.

It had continued working, the idiot greeted someone and began to talk, he reminded the idiot of someone who had helped it a long time ago—Raymond.

"… ah cayn't lyve without Him brother. Ah doan't wawnt to go backwards."

"Okay brudda, I keep to myself. Yuh have ta be strong in Him brudda."

During the time the jackass worked there, someone had said something.

"I think Dave deserves some recognition."

The idiot—at the time—didn't know exactly what that meant. Stupid idiot.

"Bambina!"

The dumb jackass still didn't see, because of the situation in a nearby city, the stupid donkey didn't trust his former co-worker: the donkey seemed to sense that the co-worker had been kicking it in the form of taking advantage of being taught kindness and charity in church—so it stayed in a familiar neighborhood for a month.

The idiot putting a stop to the complaining—the donkey had also studied his Bible, as well as a book written by a real Jewish Rabbi concerning the Old Testament, because Jesus Christ Had Heard an idiot's cry—the roommate didn't know—the donkey decided to stay with relatives while studying upstairs.

Hearing the loud, angry, belligerent female voice—it began to understand where some of that bambina woman complaining had come from.

When the donkey had helped a relative move, it had gotten its head chewed off—the dumb donkey was beginning to see.

Being late at night, it was stressed; peckerwoods were aggravating it, the idiot still had to retreat upstairs to study the bible to avoid hearing loud angry ranting—smoking out on a park bench, the idiot saw two girls walking in the park. The idiot wanted company other than loud angry women, it also turned and saw a yellow house; knowing that a poor poker face was still a problem, it smoked, then it walked home and smoked on the porch.

The dumb donkey wondered if the neighbors in the yellow house were awake.

Then it walked back into the park and smoked more, someone had walked over and kissed one of the girls.

The idiot felt better, a poor poker face combined with angry behavior had always pushed people away, yet the stupid donkey still didn't see the most important piece of the puzzle.

It prayed, then it started to walk across the park.

"Good evening sir."

He reminded the donkey of someone else who he'd worked with: yes sir.

"Hi ye doin."

"Out for a walk?"

"Can't sleep."

Unsure of what to do, it slowly turned toward a familiar house and stared.

The idiot peeked over, not wanting to be nosy, the idiot didn't say much.

One of the girls smelled good.

The idiot donkey nodded its head and walked back through the park.

The idiot wondered if the neighbors he'd grown up with were awake, but the dumb idiot didn't want to bother them, it was late.

Although an idiot donkey had a strange way of showing it, Jesus Christ the Jew Commands, Love for God, Love thy Neighbors, Love strangers.

Yet the dumb donkey didn't fully understand, or see.

The idiot because of it's loud braying jackass mouth: it prayed to His Father, The Terrible Holy Awesome Mighty Powerful Name through Jesus Christ, the idiot knew he behaved badly for a long time. The idiot found out what it feels like to be called filthy disgusting slurs and foul speech from fools: cool and calm while in the trailer, praying to Jesus Christ, seemed to repel the wicked man from attempting any violence.

Although still missing a piece of the puzzle, it still wouldn't side with fools of any kind.

Thanksgiving: a piece of the puzzle fell into place.

A relative had taken the dumb donkey aside and told it the truth.

"You have to stop hanging around him dude."

It seemed also, relatives were gathered around the poor dumb donkey, to see just exactly what the donkey was—although the fool knew he belonged to Christ—some foul people had already published a stupid book written: the reason all the relatives were gathered around it like mosquitoes.

Each frame of life flashed before the donkey's eyes—Jesus Christ showed His child the truth.

Poor dumb kid.

The whole time—someone's—sin—of pride and arrogance, and their will that they know best, an idiot had been reacting—just like a dog barking on a leash, pin the tail on the jackass then kick it.

Some people, those people, had been watching it for a very long time.

The idiot lied there and cried.

"… New Englander, I consider him friend for life."

Northern directness: friendship ended when someone got the notion to kick a gullible, stupid kid behaving like a jackass—hearing good things in church, praise Jesus Christ, King of The Jews, the dumb ass speaking with Man's Voice, The Name Made Flesh into Jesus Christ: while in the car, filthy communication had been spewed, a grown s-l-o-w l-e-a-r-n-e-r acknowledges to Christ of his former sin and stupidity: the rebuke for slurs being chanted, "Jesus Christ is Jew"—God Forgave a bag of bones—so the dumb gullible Caucasian forgives all the kicking, making merchandise, and filthy slander a 'friend' had done—also for an attempt to lead a former idiot into the hands of swine, those people who pilfered garbage from a computer.

Friendship is no longer possible. When the yoke of bondage had been revealed to an idiot by a relative, sight of this 'friend' had been made clear by Jesus Christ.

Frustration, the younger sibling had heard a "trickling down effect" of a bully, the very opposite of what Jesus Christ com-

mands: combined with loud angry belligerent provocation of a hostile bambina woman—think cabinet scraping, the 'old' kid had tried to tell the younger sibling the right way, Jesus Christ.

Unable to make him accept, free will; sadness because it's the only sibling a grown, slow learning kid will ever have.

Angry bullies that side with evil, "We're FAMILY" upon an idiot moving out of a nearby city, they aren't family, they're fools.

The wretch no longer trusted his former co-worker, the idiot wisely moved back into his own neighborhood.

The wretch studied his bible, the command to 'blot out remembrance of the wicked' would be obeyed, praise Jesus Christ the Jew.

The wretch decided to attend church, and Obey his Father, The Living God of Israel, Who Will Judge The wicked, is feared by a slow learning wretch, adoration for His Son Jesus Christ, a lawyer, is complete.

The good goals, for just one person to see that Christ Died and Rose again, just one person to hear and receive the good news; can not force any, but just truth for the benefit of others.

Just one person.

"… we're stuck together like glue … oath …"

While an 'intervention' was happening, the idiot had remembered Tunde and Denise coming down to visit, obviously, since the bearded man in the picture had said "I'll be back kiddo", then shot himself in a West Palm beach motel, a man that biologically who a grown wretch takes after physically, (lisp added) sssorry, not men!—brought a wretch into this world, a liar and a coward: the tears of humiliation poured down as the realization that those people—white trash peckerwoods with sheets on their heads, the wicked who'll be blotted out—published all that garbage, the reason, also all the rah rah 'rapping' within the junk car for the saccharin intervention. Like mosquitoes, it seemed they hovered around an idiot, who was in the process of revival, dying to all of that filthiness that not one, but two angry bambina women had drilled into it—"Well, the only example you've had to draw on was my father and I."

Guess the truth hurts for some: God put to rest, that ugly, creepy, non-pleasant brute beast. While revival was happening, the outer man dying, the woman had approached, full of asp venom under the saccharin sweetness,

"What exactly are you?"

The inarticulate wretch, under pressure dropping on it by the lost and blind,

"I'm a baby."

Switching the hearing dial off, a sneer with a grunt—reminding the wretch of just exactly who had pulled the idiot in the opposite direction of where it's body wanted to go, who had caused trouble within the town with aggressive, hostile belligerent bad behavior, pushing a lot of good people away from the idiot, causing loneliness and suffering.

The reason for this answer, everything, had to be learned all over again. What was happening within was too awesome to explain before—with the exception of the grandmother and an aunt who'd told the idiot the truth—the lost and blind who could care less about Jesus Christ, the only thing they seemed to want was to humiliate an idiot: present tense, advice to them would be given—do not side with peckerwoods—or be blotted out with them—Praise Jesus Christ The King of Kings, because the wicked do not wish to know Him—The Holy Awesome Mighty Powerful Feared Name Will be Terrible Against them.

A wretch looking at old pictures with tears streaming down—someone had arrogantly put a yoke, choke chain and made it into a brute beast.

The wicked had wanted that former beast.

It had died—Praise Jesus Christ.

In the park it had grown up in, although the wretch mostly stayed up in the room of relatives; a woman had stubbornly insisted that a wretched slow learner was falling apart—an appointment with a doctor was made. To shut the loud mouth: careful listening revealed, the woman was exactly like someone else, belligerent, persistent, obstinate.

A wretch suddenly wished that the bearded man had stayed alive to tell his side of the story—but that door was closed.

Sitting in the doctor's office: all the memories of various babysitters, in New Hampshire—someone had been loud, stubborn, and feet elsewhere—the parallel was happening with a younger sibling, all the belligerence, aggression, toxic waste dumping—several times in the idiot's life, someone had been gone. A former idiot would have to answer for sin—but the knowledge of why such hostility—"I think we need to mother him" was revealed, something that should've never happened to anyone, much less a blond haired boy had happened due to neglect.

God Forgave an idiot, so the idiot couldn't get angry, now it would be suffering for Jesus Christ.

Because someone had been a positive influence in his life—Tunde—the reason why all the 'rapping', all the switch in music, no one else wanted to see or listen.

Coolly glancing over at the angry bambina woman—Tunde had been cool, calm, and rational; an example that had saved a former supervisor from being violently attacked with a knife, instead it was seven stitches in the arm, the shred of rational thinking of not carving initials into a peckerwood's face and being sent to prison—like some 'other people' need to go. The very woman sitting next to the wretch had provoked and irritated it when it was lost, blind, suffering and dead, during the 'intervention', this seemed to be lost on her.

"... for the past year and a half, he's had a southern accent ..."

The angry woman continued to rant, former idiot behavior would not be revived again—no matter how much hostility she'd direct at her son she'd physically given birth to—not only bad mistakes—sin.

Knowing that she liked to pick fights—someone else also did this behavior—the wretch had to pray to Jesus Christ to behave calmly, and speak coolly like Tunde—any outburst of rah rah rah shtuff would only give place to her. Acknowledgment of sin to the Living God of Israel and acceptance in His Glory of Jesus Christ, The King of Jews, opposite sides of the fence.

The belligerence in the response was clear.

"He seems to think my father is gay."

"Your sister had told the truth."

Although slow learning, an idiot had noticed postures, something someone had said while the wicked had been after an idiot: "My wife has the thick sound ..."—finding out that answer—"yew list'n tae me ..."—dropped all the hostility and anger.

The realization that nothing had ever really been wrong—once the foul things had begun to happen, toxic waste being continually dumped on it, examples of bad behavior learned—with the exception of a woman who'd run the household in secret for years, encouraged a broken dead idiot to attend church—the pictures of Tunde and Denise hurt—there was something they had that had been missing from a household—Love.

The doctor asked the former idiot how he was feeling.

He responded truthfully.

"Better, We're in the New Testament of Jesus Christ."

"I didn't know that."

A former idiot hadn't told the doctor—the idiot had been slowly learning himself.

More angry belligerence from the couch, the hearing dial was set to low.

Then the doctor had spotted a truth, another unhealthy relationship, someone who'd dumped toxic waste.

"Well, you're not married to the case."

The former idiot grinned.

"Amen."

What could've saved much money was partially summed up in just that statement—a former idiot wanted to know, just exactly where the woman sitting next to him got the notion that we'd been 'married'.

"… stuck together like glue … oath …"

Praise Jesus Christ—He Is Stronger than that.

Should a former idiot find a woman—clingy isn't the type.

"Friendship ain't required."

Smiling faces: former roommates that attempted to manipulate and control a s-l-o-w-l-e-a-r-n-I-n-g, verbally inarticulate Caucasian—inarticulate is much better than angry belligerent shouting, no more of that rah rah behavior is required either. The darkness doesn't comprehend—God Sees all, fornication with a non-Christian woman—the reason a kid stayed back from going to a strip bar, instead studying the bible—Sin, defiling the temple with the dead: this has nothing to do with outward appearance, i.e. skin color—the smiling faces, prior to Thanksgiving, a.k.a. roommates—saw things a bit different than a s-l-o-w learning kid, who'd been kind to them, unknowingly.

After Thanksgiving: the hostility between God's undeserving wretch, praise Jesus Christ, the Caucasian's Master—and a roommate was clearly present.

When the sound that didn't belong in the first place had disappeared—opposite sides of the fence.

Seeing—a kid forgives former roommates: but "Friendship, ain't required."

Moving out, not much was said; the bully had demanded payment for bills. Study of the bible meant instruction for living—humility and meekness before the hateful and wicked was applied. Many things were clear to the idiot—it seemed that the former 'friend' had decided to join the wicked. Although, the former brute beast had laughed like a fool, sharing filthiness it had learned from others loading glass up north—Praise Jesus Christ, his lawyer—fools die.

While out and about, he'd seemed nervous.

Two girls behind the counter watched, they seemed to know something the idiot didn't perceive yet.

"That's awesome."

After the van had been loaded up, he spoke.

"We're friends. FAMILY."

Pulling away, the bark was unheeded.

The idiot prayed to Jesus Christ, he thanked Him for nice people who'd helped out; people across the street, someone at the temp agency, as well as two co-workers—one who the former brute beast had driven into a nearby city.

She'd given what the former idiot should've gotten more often while growing up instead of neglectful belligerence—a smack in the back of the head.

Praise Jesus Christ—side with the wicked, uh-uh!

"Only sissies and dirtbags hit women ..."

A bully, manipulating a gullible kid—booksmart, not smart when judging character or company, i.e. "Have some pizza bites bitch! Dave's a little bitch!" "Hah, hah, you got? up the what?"—spraypainted on the signs, Kaos Kids? L.B.M., on a basketball ball hoop in a park that a slow learning kid grew up in—all those who are still confused, the suggestion is you get the???? out—we're blue, wanna be red—take a vacation, far down south—who says you can't go home, right?

Although, "McFlyy!" wrote, and just too 'white and nerdy'—although not completely sure, there must be a reason someone didn't charge a slow learner for rent—making merchandise of you, while feasting with you, sporting themselves with their own deceivings—Praise Jesus Christ for His Word, endures Forever: a former roommate did tremble when realization what happened,

—"This girl has an effect on me."—

sunk in.

Maybe playing video games involving spray-paint, or books in a nerd's room—Kaos Kids!—had given someone the notion to 'tag' stop signs—Ryker's Island the solution offered for hateful criminal peckerwoods: call a former brute beast whatever you want to—just have to add it to the list of filthy communication for someone 'been caught stealing'. Think 'V', only a slow learner just doesn't have all that garbage left anymore—best to leave it all to The God of Israel, He Loves Judgment.

Praise Jesus Christ, Amen.

Besides—only sissies and dirtbags hit women: to new recruits, guess what they do—"There are no victims, only volunteers"—who's the little? now—yaaaaah!

Violent trauma: guess that's preparation H for Ryker's Island—aaaaaah!

Contrary to popular belief (lisp added) no sssir, I ssstill don't ssslep with men!—forgiveness is important, for former room-mates, just like aggressive advertisers drilling it in twice—friendship ain't required.

"... I'd shoot them in each elbow ..." "... a punch thrown into the couch ..." "... I'd been strong ..."

First, not sure strong would be the correct adjective—a former child being tyrannized, waste dumped on it, aggravated, provoked to unhealthy—carnal seething anger, sin, the bible condemns that kind of anger—the adjective of choice would be rational—Tunde: Praise Jesus Christ, it's good not to rock the boat—especially since some didn't know, but now they do—thanks to the wicked and hateful, embarrassing a nerdy Caucasian. No more of that can be fueled, a sinning wretch already has enough to answer to his Lawyer for, praise Jesus Christ.

Because of that very stunt—some would probably blame the former idiot that wrote chapters of garbage, for every school shooting that just so happens in April, on "Someone's" birth-day—Praise The Living God of The Jews, Jesus Christ, Hosanna in the Highest, Amen—April should be for Him, Crucifixion, Resurrection, Amen—not "someone's birthday".

In a bar, a couple former classmates had tried to help the slow learner, so bringing back all of that garbage that a couple of bambina women stirred up—that's not going to happen again, that's lunacy to stay angry at children—hopefully they know Jesus Christ. Much better to speak the truth, present tense, a former idiot doesn't say too much, or even like to talk.

A woman that had visited a former dead thing in the hospital had said—"the people you hate don't know it, or don't care"—just like a grown kid doesn't care that those people, (pinky extended) aaaaah, hate a grown up kid's guts—the publishing of garbage in an attempt to stir up trouble was the action: the cause, because Jesus Christ The King of the Jews guided a former brute beast away from angry, 'unnatural' bambina women, angry, because a kid wouldn't wear a sheet and sexually prefer men like them, yaaaaaah!

Knowing that filthy behavior—formerly a brute beast—drew the attention of those people, peckerwoods—only the best behavior possible for each day, all that past is forgotten.

Praise Jesus Christ, a slow learner's lawyer—The Name Who Sent Him Respects no one.

Especially not a former brute beast.

Driving down 81—all the rah rah loud behavior in the car had stopped, the music had also stopped. Since fools seek attention, the struggle now was a former fool seemed to be put on display for all to see and spit on—the Author of the bible commands humility and meekness, in a country that seems to have forgotten Who blessed it. All the gossipy stuff that exits a large animal's backside with horns who charges at red sheets—"Toro"—spray painted on a stop sign; rumors from a false friend had done damage.

One of the reasons a former brute beast fool enjoyed the scenic drive down the road—without all of that rah rah bad behavior.

Like all the 'old world' ignorance, that rah rah reaction to being kicked, pained, and aggravated by some would be left behind.

The city of Nashville seemed to jump up, pulling off I-40 West, a slow learning kid merged into city traffic.

A cousin nodded his head, seeing a former fool pull right into the city—although a kid had stayed in the North Eastern part of the state, any who interacted with the slow learning kid were polite.

A couple girls smiled, the former idiot smiled back.

He didn't get 'injured'.

Staying at different hotels, a kid read, and prayed—he knew he was still ice cold, not a good example, i.e., poor church attendance.

A slow process of growing, every bit read was applied—still aggravatingly s-l-o-w, the former foul behavior was fading.

The slow learner liked the city, more girls had smiled, the former idiot smiled back.

After getting the required paperwork, a kid had found a job.

Starting work; the thick country sound was in his ears, both Caucasians and Africans.

Not saying much, a kid listened to them—key phrases presented themselves. Although s-l-o-w l-e-a-r-n-I-n-g, the former fool silently prayed to Jesus Christ in Thanks.

It seemed both co-workers liked to talk.

"… I'm just a good ole boy."

After work, soreness was the main focus, a grown kid lied down in rest and prayer.

The former idiot didn't say much, his co-workers were polite; after being aggravated, pained, tyrannized, toxic waste dumped on; all the aggressive loud reaction was allowed to fade, a grown kid cared less whether or not who liked it—prayers were offered in silence to God through His Son, Jesus Christ for co-workers.

After work, a grown kid stayed in his hotel room. Although a poor man's hotel, a broken Caucasian kid had liked staying—the cares and fears of the world, Praise Jesus Christ—with His Help, blocked out.

Early in life with foul circumstances, continual bad behavior—toxic dumping, paining, tyrannizing, 'smiling faces'—a grown up kid had some understanding of being broken, the only other direction to move was up.

People in general were polite, they didn't pry.

Although his co-workers might not have realized, being quiet and helping out was about the best a former brute beast—creepy, ugly, non-pleasant thing could do.

Praying for their souls Was done in silence.

It doesn't have to be loud.

On his third day, the grown kid heard.

"I'm just a good ole boy."

"Super Dave!"

Briefly stopping: within, the knowledge of what, chapters weren't just in it's own state, but smeared all across the country—and who: those people, sissies, dirtbags, unnatural women—brute beasts, creepy, ugly, non-pleasant, the gossipy people that spread slander about a nerdy Caucasian kid that—Praise Jesus Christ—refused to wear a sheet over the head, and sexually prefer men like them.

Concerning 'pop culture', if gossip is all offered—Praise Jesus Christ, than a grown kid wants no part in it.

Gossip all they want: a grown kid isn't running for office.

Although not saying much, or listening to much music anymore—the music that Tunde had played is still enjoyed, and although still not putting a sheet over the head and sexually preferring men, very rarely Johnny Cash is listened to in a headset. Sadly, many people hate when a Yankee Caucasian learns good things from other people who are different—Tunde, Raymond, etc.—the world hates when a former brute beast learns from the One Who Made it, and All things, Who Died not for some, but for All—Praise Jesus Christ, Hosanna In The Highest.

At work, the moving job was brutal, yet the kid grinned—although some of the office workers being moved; a couple girls had smiled, the former idiot smiled back; due to filthy chapters and sssssissiesss sssspreading the gay rumorssss, a couple had erred concerning their judgments about a slow learning kid—(lisp added) no sssir, I don't sssleep with men. An ice cold example, silent prayer while office furniture was moved—Gordon's words were silently chanted along with scripture.

A kid wouldn't be ashamed.

Sore and tired in the hotel, a kid studied the bible, and prayed, some had tried to aggravate and provoke—Judgment Is Left To The Most High God—The Name Who Sent His Son, Jesus Christ for the World He Made, Amen, Hallelujah.

While relaxing on the bed, old School R&B played in a kid's ears—grins at the pictures helped make the kid forget about all the ignorance, from all angles. Not trying to change anyone, it seemed a nice place to visit, yet it seemed to be red. If any wanted to be red, fine—not sssssissy ultra extremist red—some people in a kid's home state needed to be recognized and reminded that it's blue. Thinking about being the town idiot, there's no excuse for sin and bad behavior, there also needs to be some restructured thought on behalf of it's always interesting to hear new filthy forms of communication, exercise of free will, blessing when others revile and curse, praise Jesus Christ.

Concerning red vs. blue: although a former idiot fool brute beast, always was blue, pictures prove it. Not mixing up with politics, worship any other than Jesus Christ, i.e.—state, nation, money—that notion needs to be canceled as well despite being a lousy example.

Lying on the bed, a grown kid in the very least is like a relative in this respect—stubbornly holding to Jesus Christ, regardless of who or how many 'spit.'

A kid relaxed, forgetting about all the effects a loud mouth caused.

He'd liked his co-workers, a former fool had pinched his nose while talking.

His co-worker shook his hand: seemed that some in a former idiot's home state needed to be recognized, reminded (Slapped, lisp added) that gossssipy grown up little unnatural girlssss should be sent to their rooms—Ryker's Island—if they missssbehave, hoooo, yaaaaaah!

He read and prayed.

"… Doesn't sound Jamaican …"

While helping them move—a grown kid's co-workers looked like linebackers. More awareness, the knowledge of trying to change others is pointless—it wouldn't be long before a kid went back; some needed to know, if you want to be red, head down the road.

Concerning any of that rah rah shtuff—knowing just who the 'demographic' would be punished first—cool and rational, Tunde, was much better than impulsive hot-headed behavior that causes trouble: angry unnatural women—those people.

No behaviors, to cause any others trouble including Caucasians—those people would be denied—a struggle in itself for a former brute beast filled full of garbage doctrine. Because of Tunde, it wouldn't have sided with those people, swine, despite temptation to dish out a dose of the former wrath and fury to a baldhead with orange flame tattoos, hanging on some kid filling his head full of baloney such as 'racial purity' and how God Loves only some, while others are lower class; instead, slaps to their ugly faces will be given liberally: advice to be cool headed is given, let the wicked destroy themselves—why not give them recognition, those people deserve.

Praise Jesus Christ, Amen.

The Name Who Sent Him to the Cross Sees All.

The kid helped his co-workers, praying for them both.

Although quitting employment—no past feeling of failure stuck in the mind, what was needed was heard.
They were polite, girls had smiled.
A kid began to feel human again.
Forgive and forget.
One day at a time.

During the drive back, the junk car had broken down.
Not the best decision maker, a s-l-o-w learner had managed to keep cool—an example that had been missing for a long time, nothing but garbage had been dumped on it.
Sitting in the bus station praying, a girl sat near.
During the bus ride, a slow learner relaxed, then arrived at the train station.
While walking—someone talked with the former idiot.
Beginning to like her, a grown kid was still awkward and nervous—he wanted to be on the same train and head to Philedelphia—but it was the later train.
He'd grinned anyway—it was nice to have girls talk instead of filthy communication—"Go F*** yourself motherf****r"—unable to control the ignorant from spitting their wisdom, the best was careful watching within—silence and prayer—a filthy communication sheet is marked: a nerdy reading Caucasian is always interested in brand new names, labels, slurs, judgments, gossips, and other forms of filth from any who wish to use their free will that God Gave them.
Praise Jesus Christ, Amen.
While talking with the girl in the train station—the ignorance had come from two adolescent Caucasian girls—seems the parents

are already starting them young, to be unnatural 'women' like their older brothers.

Praise Jesus Christ—although being broken is unpleasant—no where to go except up—just wisdom, Praise the Lord Jesus Christ, for the benefit of any others, no matter the outward appearance.

All that former wrath and garbage that the ignorant love—Only with Jesus Christ could a former idiot forgive and let go.

While calling a service station from where a former brute beast grew up—talking with relatives tested the former idiot fool.

That toxic waste—provocation to anger, belligerence, loud, sharp cold edge was dished out—only because of revival in Jesus Christ could a former brute beast keep cool and calm: the continued toxicity the very reason why—respect for the woman who physically gave birth was first and foremost.

Since Love is behavior—Truth of Jesus Christ Was given to the woman—refusal the result; sad, yet no sense in telling any who refuse to listen, the result being torn by others on the opposite side of the fence—Praise The Living God of Israel for Free Will.

He Knows who Belongs to Him and who does not.

After making phone calls—the former idiot and a relative drove down a familiar road—I-81—to pick up a junk car.

The relative drove—some stubborn gibberish had to be blocked out—then the former brute beast drove.

Although they no longer said much to each other, there seemed to be a truce while driving in the car—it certainly wasn't all of someone's fault, a s-l-o-w learner had sinned, made bad choices—The God of Israel Gives what is needed—Correction, when He Corrects, it hurts—a former brute beast is extremely glad of his lawyer, Jesus Christ.

While driving down, the former idiot wished someone would listen to the Good News—it didn't seem likely.

A former idiot didn't even want someone to share the fate of the wicked—those people, who in their attempts to force a kid to 'kill himself' also put a grown kid's relatives on the spot—the reason those people are being recognized, slapped like little?'s, yaaaaaaah!

Best to leave Judgment of those people to God—He Loves Judgment, everything—including vengeance—is His.

Praise the lawyer, Jesus Christ, Amen.

One day at a time.

Bibliography

Rabbi Joseph Telushkin. *You Shall Be Holy Vol. 1* © 2006

Rabbi Joseph Telushkin. *Biblical Literacy* © 1997

Neil T. Anderson. *Victory over the Darkness* © 1990

Timothy White. *Catch a fire: The Life of Bob Marley* © 1983, 1989, 1991, 1992, 1994, 1996, 1998

Dore Gold. *Hatred's Kingdom* © 2003

978-0-595-46018-2
0-595-46018-6